About this version of *The Imitation of Christ*:

Many translators have attempted to convey the meaning of *The Imitation of Christ* from the fifteenth-century Latin of Thomas à Kempis into English. But none has so brilliantly succeeded in capturing every nuance of meaning, every cadence of expression, the spirit of freshness and even ebullience that permeates the great classic as did Richard Whitford, whose translation first appeared around 1530. Here was the perfect rendering of a thing of perfection.

Indeed, so far-reaching were the effects of this translation that only now are scholars beginning to appreciate its tremendous influence on the mainstream of the English language. Appearing as it did at a crucially formative stage in the development of our language, its effects have hitherto been obscured. Happily, recent research has set Whitford's magnificent translation in its proper perspective as a source of much of the beauty of the English language as well as a superb translation of a timeless classic.

But with the passage of more than four centuries and the consequent growth and diversification of the English language, many of the expressions used by Whitford which were perfectly valid and meaningful in his day became archaic and meaningless to readers in the twentieth century. Consequently, a new version which would retain the limpid beauty and pure devotion of Whitford's translation, while adapting it to the ear and mind of the modern reader, was undertaken by Father Harold C. Gardiner, S.J., the literary editor of America. The result is this Image Book version which makes available for millions of present day readers *The Imitation of Christ* in a modern form while preserving the spirit and beauty of the magnificent meditations by means of which "we will truly be illumined and be delivered from all blindness of the heart."

THE IMITATION OF CHRIST

Thomas à Kempis

*A Modern Version
based on the English translation
made by* RICHARD WHITFORD
around the year 1530

Edited with introduction by
HAROLD C. GARDINER, S.J.

IMAGE BOOKS
DOUBLEDAY
NEW YORK LONDON TORONTO SYDNEY AUCKLAND

AN IMAGE BOOK
PUBLISHED BY DOUBLEDAY
a division of Bantam Doubleday Dell Publishing Group, Inc.
1540 Broadway, New York, New York 10036

IMAGE, DOUBLEDAY, and the portrayal of a deer drinking from
a stream are trademarks of Doubleday, a division of Bantam
Doubleday Dell Publishing Group, Inc.

First Image edition published September 1955
by special arrangement with Doubleday, a division of
Bantam Doubleday Dell Publishing Group, Inc.
This Image edition published December 1989.

IMPRIMATUR
✠ FRANCIS CARDINAL SPELLMAN
ARCHBISHOP OF NEW YORK

ISBN 0-385-02861-X

Library of Congress Catalog Card Number 55-9752

On a day in 1392, Thomas Haemerken, a German boy of some twelve years, knocked on the door of Florent Radewijns in the town of Deventer, in the Low Countries. He had made the journey from his native Kempen, fifteen miles northwest of present-day Dusseldorf. His older brother John had made the same trip some years earlier, in order to join a small community founded by Gerard Groote and now directed by Radewijns, where Latin studies and the copying and illustrating of manuscripts flourished.

We can somewhat picture the scene—the cobbled street of the medieval town, the simple and quaint homes lining it, and before the door a little German boy, perhaps wearing the clogs we associate with the peasants and burghers, sturdy, healthy, perhaps a bit shy, but quiet and determined. Descriptions of Thomas in later life refer to him as of medium build, of healthy complexion somewhat dark, of quiet but firm disposition, of studious and reflective nature.

Even at this early age Thomas yearned for education and the quiet life of reading and study. His favorite motto is said to have been: "I sought for rest but never found it, save in a little corner with a little book." Perhaps he also felt even so early the call to the religious or the monastic life. Which of these two impulses was the more urgent we will never know. But what an important day it was for the whole history of Christian life and asceticism, even for the course of Western literature.

Thomas had been born at Kempen in 1379/80, the son of John and Gertrude Haemerken (the family name means "little hammer"). His father was a blacksmith

5

and his mother ran a school for small children. He attended classes—probably his mother's—until he left for Deventer. Seven years after his arrival, he determined to enter the religious life. His older brother was prior of the monastery of Mount St. Agnes, at Agnetenberg, beyond the walls of the city of Zwolle, but the Rule forbade two brothers to live in the same community, without special dispensation. Permission was granted, an official recognition of the good character of both the brothers. Thomas pronounced the three vows of religion—poverty, chastity, and obedience—in 1406/7 and was ordained a priest in 1413 at the age of thirty-three.

In 1425 he was appointed sub-prior of the monastery, and was also entrusted with the training of the novices. For a brief time he was procurator (treasurer) of the house, but it was soon recognized that he had little talent for this kind of administration.

The world in which he found himself in these years was a particularly confused and bewildered one. When we speak of the little German boy knocking on a door in a "quaint" Low Country village in 1392 to seek a life of study and peace, it sounds quite remote and idyllic. It was not at all remote to Thomas, of course, nor was the world in which he lived idyllic. The very foundations of the Church—and hence the Western civilization—seemed to be shaken and crumbling. At the end of the fourteenth and at the beginning of the fifteenth centuries, Philip the Fair and Pope Boniface VIII were at odds, and the Emperor Louis of Bavaria fought with three Popes: John XXII, Benedict XII, and Clement VI. Christian people were trying to find a true successor to St. Peter, the first Pope, among two and sometimes three "anti-Popes."

Nor was the bewilderment of the day confined to the world of politics and high diplomacy. Monasteries and convents were often torn by inner dissensions; the tumult of the outside world made its way into places and souls where the peace of God should have reigned.

6

Religion, it may be said, was in not too healthy a state. Still, as has often happened in the Church of Christ, in the midst of the hurly-burly and the spiritual torpor, God raised up great and noble souls: a St. Catherine of Siena in Italy; Henry Suso and Ludolph of Saxony in Germany; Jean Charlier de Gerson in France; and, in the Low Countries, the followers of the "modern devotion," such as Gerard Groote.

This last group, with which Thomas of Kempen became associated that day in 1392, did not constitute or join a religious order, but simply determined to live their lives as nearly as possible in imitation of the lives of the early Christians. As the movement grew, many affiliated to it still lived in their own homes, but endeavored to preserve the spirit; others, especially priests, lived in community. Their character is perhaps best denoted by the simple name they chose to go under: "The Brothers of the Common Life." Their teachings were called the "modern devotion," by which they wished to be distinguished from those who were delving too much, they thought, into a pretentious mysticism. One of their chief aims was not merely to deepen the religious life as a cure for the widespread religious laxity of the times, but also to promote sound learning. By the end of the fifteenth century, schools of the Brotherhood had sprung up all over Germany and the Netherlands, and such a man as Erasmus had come under their influence. It is worth noting that the influence of their teaching resulted in a period in which Flemish prose is said to have been at a stage of remarkable purity.

The Brotherhood was not looked on with admiring eyes from all directions. They taught freely, for the love of God; they were not allowed to ask for or receive alms, but worked for their daily bread. Hence, not a few vested interests, religious and civil alike, were quick to dub them dangerous reformers. However, they were approved by Pope St. Gregory XI in 1376 and gradually grew to enjoy the support of such men as the great Cardinal of Cusa, Nicholas.

In 1384, however, when Gerard Groote lay dying at the early age of forty-four, he felt that his Brotherhood needed a firmer and more stable organization, and so he urged them to adopt the Rule of the Canons Regular of St. Augustine. When Thomas, therefore, entered the monastery of Mount St. Agnes and took his vows, he became a religious in the strict sense of the word, though, of course, the monastic life he embraced still preserved the spirit of the Brotherhood.

Groote's desires were first put into effect by the foundation of a house of the Order at Windesheim, some four miles south of Zwolle, in 1387, and it is from the chronicles of these two establishments, at Windesheim and Zwolle, that most of the facts of Thomas' life are discovered. Deventer, where he began his studies, was an independent branch. By the end of the eighteenth century, only two branches were left; the Reformation had swept nearly eighty others out of existence, even Deventer, which at one time had numbered 2,000 students. The last two foundations were suppressed on November 14, 1811, by Napoleon. The last surviving brother died at Zevenaar in 1854.

Contemporary turmoil came directly before Thomas' eyes in 1422, when the canons of the four churches in Utrecht designated Rudolph of Diepholt to succeed the deceased Frederick of Blankenhem to the episcopal see. When Pope Martin V learned that Rudolph was illiterate and almost a moron, he ignored the designation and appointed Seuder of Culenborg. But the people wanted Rudolph and refused to accept Seuder. The Pope promptly placed the diocese under interdict—that is, the sacraments were withheld (though they were always available in cases of grave necessity, as at danger of death); the people were to be barred from Communion, confession, from hearing Mass, and the like, until they obeyed. The citizens of Utrecht then demanded that the

8

clergy either administer the sacraments to them or get out.

The Order to which Thomas belonged chose exile rather than disobedience to the Pope, and moved, on June 11, 1429, to the monastery of Lunenkerk near Harlingen. His brother John's health was failing, and was apparently worsened by the circumstances of the move. He died at Bethany, near Arnheim, three years later. Thus, Thomas knew from intimate and agonizing experience—he was very close to the brother some fifteen years his senior—what the religious disorders of the time meant and could lead to. This is probably one reason why the pages of *The Imitation* are so sincere, so convincing in their tone of immediate experience, rather than seeming to echo spiritual teaching which is good and sound but rather remote and theoretical. Thomas knew the world from which he was so strongly to recommend withdrawal—though that withdrawal must be understood as Thomas meant it, not as some commentators have read their own meaning into it.

After his brother's death, Thomas held various other posts in the monastery and in 1448 was elected subprior for the second time. Then, for the next twenty years, his was the quiet life of student, counselor, copyist, and writer. From his pen, in addition to *The Imitation*, came a remarkable quantity of work (of which *The Imitation* comprises only about one-tenth), including sermons, treatises for the instructions of the novices and monks, devotional works, and two biographies—of St. Lydwine, virgin, and of Gerard Groote.

He died on July 25, 1471, "having completed," says the Chronicle of Mount St. Agnes, "on the feast of St. James the Greater, the 92nd year of his age, the 63rd of his religious life, and the 58th of his priesthood." He was buried in the monastery grounds, but two centuries after the Reformation, by which time the monastery was long destroyed, his remains were transferred to Zwolle, where they rest in the Church of St. Michael. In 1897 a monument was erected over them, built through subscriptions collected from all over the world. The inscription reads: "*Honori, non memoriae, Thomae Kempensis, cujus nomen perennius quam monumentum*"—"To the honor, not the memory, of Thomas à Kempis, whose name is more enduring than any monument."

His real monument, of course, is *The Imitation* or *Following of Christ*, the widest-read and best-loved religious book in the world, with the exception only of the Bible. Since its completion, around 1427, *The Imitation* has literally traversed the ages and covered the continents. As early as 1450, more than 250 manuscript copies had been made; today, more than 700 are known. It was printed in type for the first time in 1472; another edition from type, appearing in Venice in 1483, was reprinted fifty times before 1500. By 1779, no less than 1,800 editions and translations could be counted. Since then, there is no computing how often the book has been translated and edited.

Yet, Thomas à Kempis' masterpiece has achieved the dubiously pleasant distinction of having been attributed to almost everyone under the sun except to him. Over the centuries, some twenty-five different "authors" have been identified, including St. Bernard, St. Bonaventure, Ludolph of Saxony, John Gersen, Jean de Gerson, and Gerard Groote. In reality, it does not matter much who wrote its golden message; scholars may search and argue, but the reader wants the feast, no matter who serves it.

There is no need here to delve deeply into the question of authorship. The most ancient manuscripts of *The Imitation* carry no author's name. In 1434, when John de Bellerive presented a copy to the Brothers of the Common Life of the monastery at Weinbach, near Cologne, he spoke as if the author wished to be unknown: "He did not wish to name himself, and that will win him an eternal recompense; but Jesus knows his name well." Thomas is named by others as author only beginning with a manuscript of 1447; but from then on there is a mounting tide of manuscripts which contain such attributions as "This book was made by Thomas à Kempis, regular of Mount St. Agnes near Zwolle."

The two others whose possible authorship has been seriously considered are Jean de Gerson (1363–1429), Chancellor of the University of Paris, and Groote. The Gerson tradition goes back to the fifteenth century, and is based on the appearance of his name on a manuscript of 1460 and on printed editions many times thereafter. Modern research rather strongly rules him out, for the reason that *The Imitation* is clearly the work of a monk (Gerson was a diocesan priest); that its style matches that of other works by Thomas, even in Dutch idioms; and that its author was steeped in the "modern devotion" of the Brotherhood of the Common Life and relied heavily on their favorite Scriptural passages and those from St. Augustine and St. Bernard which appealed to the group around Windesheim.

It was not until 1924 that the claim for Gerard Groote was given much scholarly attention. The grounds adduced for his authorship are based on a 1441 manuscript which gives evidence of having been written in Thomas' own hand and which closes: "Finished and completed in the year of our Lord 1441 by the hand of Brother Thomas Kempis, at Mount St. Agnes, near Zwolle." *The Imitation* was completed long before this, and Thomas may have been making another copy of his own work—a practise not at all rare in those days. But others claim that the action proves him to be merely a copyist. They also point out that in this 1441 manuscript the treatise on the Eucharist becomes the fourth book, when the progression of thought and style seem to demand that it be the third; a transcriber might make such an error with none too familiar material. Finally, they say, the key doctrine of *The Imitation*, withdrawal into interior solitude, was pre-eminently the doctrine on which Groote based his own spiritual life and founded the Brotherhood. This theory, however, collides with the fact that, of the 700 extant manuscripts, not one carries Groote's name, and no chronicler or author of the Windesheim federation of monasteries and convents ever attributes *The Imitation* to their own founder.

One difficulty I have never seen discussed is Thomas' age when he wrote *The Imitation*. At first glance, the book would seem to enshrine the meditations of an old —at least, a mature—man. It is, some are inclined to think, not a book for the reading of the young. So, the author must have been a man whose youth was far behind him, else he would have spoken more in accents understandable to youth—the youth of his day and the youth of any age. If Thomas wrote *The Imitation*, he completed it when he was about forty-seven. At first blush, this seems preposterous—until we remember a recent occurrence. Thomas Merton was twenty-six when he entered the Trappist monastery at Gethsemani. This modern Thomas had not come up the straight and direct way of his namesake; he had wandered, searching and questing, along ways that Thomas of Kempen would never have envisioned. Yet Thomas Merton, in his *Seven Storey Mountain*, tells the same tale that the earlier Thomas told—the tale of the restless heart and the Hound of Heaven. If Thomas Merton of the twentieth century could tell that tale at the age of thirty-three, why could not another Thomas, of the fourteenth century, have told it at the age of forty-seven? After all, an Augustine told it at forty-six.

The Imitation was first translated from Latin into English in 1460 by an unknown translator who omitted the fourth book. This was a manuscript version. The first English version to be printed was made in 1502 by William Atkinson, a Cambridge scholar; this, again, contained only the first three books. In 1503, Lady Margaret Beaufort, mother of King Henry VII and patron of St. John Fisher, translated the fourth book from a French version. A combined Atkinson-Beaufort translation was reprinted many times in the early sixteenth century. In 1530 appeared the Whitford version, which is the basis of this present offering.

Briefly, the life of Richard Whitford ran as follows. He was born about 1476, near Holywell in Flintshire, Wales. He was elected a Fellow of Queens' College, Cambridge, in 1495. The following year, he obtained a leave of absence for five years to accompany William Blount, fourth Lord of Mountjoy, to the Continent as chaplain and confessor—where and when he was ordained is not known. He returned to England in 1498 and soon after was appointed chaplain to Richard Foxe, Bishop of Winchester. About 1507 he entered the Brigittine monastery of Syon House, Ilesworth, Middlesex (he refers to himself wryly as "the wretch of Syon"). There he began a fruitful career of writing, ending with his death in 1555. His devotional treatises were widely read, and noted for the exceptional charm and appeal of their English style. These qualities are beautifully evident in his version of *The Imitation*, which the *Dictionary of National Biography* has called "in style and feeling, the finest rendering into English of the famous original." I must apologize, therefore, for having had to change his pure and limpid expressions from time to time to make them better adapted to the ear and the mind of the modern reader.

The most scholarly edition of the Whitford version is the truly epoch-making work which Rev. Edward J. Klein prepared for the Early English Text Society in 1939. Among the beauties of this rendering, Fr. Klein points out the simplicity and directness, the cadences of the speech which echo the liturgy and seem to have caught the rhythms of the monastic chant, and the spirit of freshness and even ebullience that runs through all. An interesting point is Whitford's fondness for the words "merry" and "glad." If in them he is faithfully catching the spirit of the original, Thomas apparently was not quite the gloomy man preaching a doctrine of anti-social withdrawal some commentators would have us think he was.

The literary influence of Whitford has not received the attention it deserves. This field has only recently been opened up by the researches of Fr. Klein, though it had been hinted at by such men as R. W. Chambers in his *On the Continuity of English Prose from Alfred to More and His School* (Oxford University Press, 1932). The reason why Chambers and other scholars had not been able to see the influence of the Whitford version was that it had been consistently misdated. Until Fr. Klein's correction, which definitely establishes the date as 1530, all references placed it in 1556.

What is the significance of this? There was a great danger, in the early sixteenth century, that English prose would go the way of excessive latinization, of pretense and posturing such as was later to mark the *Euphues* of John Lyly. One great corrective, however, was at work —the writings of the authors of books of devotion. They had resisted the impulse to ornament their English style; they kept it clear and simple and fresh, and it is to them more than to any other single influence that we owe the flexibility and richness of our language today. This matter has been gone into at considerable length by Professor Chambers, but it is still generally unrecognized in most histories of English literature.

A prime figure among these writers was St. Thomas More. There is, in fact, good reason for calling him the "father" of English prose as we now know it. Whitford and More were good friends. This is attested to, for example, by a letter to Whitford from Erasmus, written on the occasion of Erasmus' second visit to England. Speaking of More and himself, Erasmus says to Whitford: "Both of us you equally love; to both you are equally dear." And More almost certainly knew the Whitford version of *The Imitation*. If he did, his impeccable taste and keen judgment would have seen that here was a gem of English style. What more likely, accordingly, than that Whitford's cadences would have affected More and helped sharpen his own style, which was in turn to shape the direction of the English language?

Whitford's influence can be traced in still another direction, less conjectural and more far-reaching. His version was frequently printed through the sixteenth century, had a wide audience with both readers and writers, and without question was well known by those who prepared the 1611 translation of the Bible. These translators were certainly affected, says Fr. Klein, "by its lucid style, simple, vivid and fresh. It is, to use an expression of Whitford, 'a quick-springing well' whence the main-stream of the English language has drawn so much of its beauty and its life."

The Imitation had considerable literary influence in another way than style. Thomas DeQuincey, for instance, praised the charm of its use of Scripture (there are, by the way, some 850 Scriptural passages either quoted or alluded to in the four books); Charles Kingsley summarized it as "the school for many a noble soul"; Samuel Johnson, Thomas Carlyle, and others have spoken in like vein.

But the book has a particular message for each reader, an inspiring, a positive message.

In spite of Whitford's preference for the "merry" outlook, the book has often been called pessimistic, anti-intellectual, defeatist, and negative. Speaking of the "modern devotion" which was behind its writing, Fr. Philip Hughes says in his *History of the Church*, (Vol. III, pp. 216–217): "The most notable insufficiency was that nowhere . . . was piety related to doctrine, which is as much as to say that about much of it there is nothing specifically, necessarily, Catholic. . . . The absence of any care to relate piety to those revealed doctrines which the Church was divinely founded to set forth is the more serious because it was deliberate. Not, of course, that these writers were indifferent to Catholic doctrine or hostile to it. They were, all of them, excellent Catholics, as whole in faith as in charity or in zeal; they would presuppose a dogmatic foundation, known and accepted. But they were Catholics in violent reaction against the fashionable spirituality of their time—or rather, against its excesses."

This, as Fr. Hughes goes on to establish, is a dangerous state of affairs, for when piety is cut away from doctrinal foundation, it tends to become sentimental or worse. He states: "Once the direction of so delicate a thing as the *devotio moderna* passes into the hands of those unlearned in theology, all manner of deviation is possible. It can become a cult of what is merely naturally good, a thing no worse—but no more spiritual—than, say, the cult of kindness, courtesy, tidiness and the like. And what the master, unwittingly, is soon really teaching is himself; he is the hero his disciples are worshipping; there are, in the end, as many Christianities as there are masters, and chaos begins its reign."

This is very true and very wisely said, and it ought to be kept in mind especially by one who comes to *The Imitation* for the first time. The little book is not the whole of the Catholic faith; it represents a very small section of it, and that section is not dogmatic; it is not even notably intellectual. Fr. Hughes' remarks apply more to the entire movement than to this particular literary expression of it. Undoubtedly, this type of lack of care for the dogmatic foundations of piety did have an influence on thinking of the sort that paved the way for the Reformation. To accuse Thomas, however, of being a forerunner of the great revolt—as has been done by some (for example, by Canon Henry Parry Liddon, in his 1889 edition of *The Imitation*)—is to ignore the sturdy devotion to the Church manifest in all his writings.

One reason why *The Imitation* is admittedly limited in scope and in doctrinal foundation is that it was written *by a monk for monks.* This is not to say that members of a monastic order ought not to have sound doctrinal bases for their preaching and writing, but it does explain to some extent what will strike the new reader as a rather narrow point of view. So, for example, when Thomas is talking about the avoidance of "personal friendships," he is advising the monks to avoid what spiritual writers call "particular friendships" among persons living in community—those friendships which would be so exclusive that they would freeze others out, and thus be a great hindrance to the charity that ought to exist among all. Certainly, all we know about Thomas indicates that he was anything but a cold and aloof person, and his closeness to his brother shows that he was not insensitive to the ties of kindred and friendship.

Again, a tone of undue severity crops up from time to time in the translation. I have not changed all of these expressions, for I wished to keep as much as possible of the flavor of the lovely Whitford version. But I feel that Whitford at times chose, in translating, a word which, in modern English, makes Thomas sound overly forbidding. Take the word "vile," for instance, which Thomas used frequently in connection with "corruptible" in reference to the body. The Latin is *"vilis,"* and its first meaning is simply "what can be purchased of little price, of little worth." Our modern meaning of "repellent, disgusting" is thoroughly out of context here—unless, of course, we have been brought up on the fable that all monks despised the body. They didn't; they recognized it for what it is, the lovely handiwork of God, but still a thing to be kept in its place, precisely because, in comparison with the soul, it is indeed of little worth.

It may be, too, that Thomas' anti-intellectualism has been stressed too much. He does, indeed, speak of the vanity of human knowledge, and seems to disparage all learning save the knowledge that one, of oneself, is worth nothing. Perhaps the most famous phrase of *The Imitation* is: "I had rather feel compunction of heart for my sins than only know the definition of compunction." What would be wrong, one is tempted to ask, with both feeling compunction and being able to define it? However, in other passages, Thomas speaks of the legitimacy of inquiry and speculation, warning only that presumption and pride must be avoided in the intellectual search. One practical and historical reason for suspecting that Thomas and others of the Windesheim foundation were probably not the anti-intellectuals they are sometimes made out to be is that the schools for poor boys there and at Zwolle flourished and had an influence on such men as Erasmus. Granted that these schools probably taught not much more than grammar, writing, and reading, the readiness of the monks to propagate worldly knowledge to this extent argues that they did not hold knowledge as such suspect.

The Imitation breathes a spirit of humility and peace as well as a salutary fear. If Thomas insists strongly on compunction for sins, and a filial fear of the God whom we have offended, he does not forget that the goal of such compunction and fear is Christian confidence and joy. In this, though he does not explain it as a worked-out theory, he is perfectly orthodox. Christian life has two sides, shall we say, or two aspects: mistrust of ourselves, a proper diffidence in our own powers to avoid sin and grow in grace; and a rooted confidence in the grace of God, with which all things are possible to us. If this is kept in mind as *The Imitation* is read and pondered, the reader will begin to see how golden the volume is; it is to be taken, not as a complete explanation of the Catholic faith, but as a series of meditations to deepen one's interior life.

One of Thomas' own statements recommends: "We ought to seek in Holy Scripture ghostly profit rather than curiosity of style." The same admonition may be issued to the reader of this modernized version. The fact remains—at least, I hope it does—that even through the adaptation there still shines some of the beauty of Whitford's style, as well as Thomas' meaning. The reader will certainly not be brushing aside Thomas' caution if he seeks first "ghostly" or spiritual profit, while also being aware that he is becoming familiar with an English classic, even if at one remove, through this modernization of Whitford's masterpiece.

May this book prove to all readers a "quick-springing well" of "ghostly profit" and of delight in the wealth and beauty of our English tongue.

HAROLD C. GARDINER, S.J.

Campion House, New York
February 19, 1955

BOOK II

Admonitions Leading to the Inner Life

BOOK III

The Inward Speaking of Christ to a Faithful Soul

BOOK IV

Which Treats Especially of the Sacrament of the Altar

BOOK I

Admonitions Useful for a Spiritual Life

1. Of the Imitation or Following of Christ and the Despising of All Vanities of the World

He who follows Me, says Christ our Saviour, walks not in darkness, for he will have the light of life. These are the words of our Lord Jesus Christ, and by them we are admonished to follow His teachings and His manner of living, if we would truly be enlightened and delivered from all blindness of heart.

Let all the study of our heart be from now on to have our meditation fixed wholly on the life of Christ, for His holy teachings are of more virtue and strength than the words of all the angels and saints. And he who through grace has the inner eye of his soul opened to the true beholding of the Gospels of Christ will find in them hidden manna.

It is often seen that those who hear the Gospels find little sweetness in them; the reason is that they do not have the spirit of Christ. So, if we desire to have a true understanding of His Gospels, we must study to conform our life as nearly as we can to His.

What avail is it to a man to reason about the high, secret mysteries of the Trinity if he lack humility and so displeases the Holy Trinity? Truly, it avails nothing. Deeply inquisitive reasoning does not make a man holy or righteous, but a good life makes him beloved by God.

I would rather feel compunction of heart for my sins than merely know the definition of compunction. If you know all the books of the Bible merely by rote and all the sayings of the philosophers by heart, what will it profit you without grace and charity? All that is in the world is vanity except to love God and to serve Him only. This is the most noble and the most excellent wisdom that can be in any creature: by despising the world to draw daily nearer and nearer to the kingdom of heaven.

It is therefore a great vanity to labor inordinately for worldly riches that will shortly perish or to covet honor or any other inordinate pleasures or fleshly delights in this life, for which a man after this life will be sorely and grievously punished. How great a vanity it also is to desire a long life and to care little for a good life; to heed things of the present and not to provide for things that are to come; to love things that will shortly pass away and not to haste to where joy is everlasting. Have this common proverb often in your mind: The eye is not satisfied or pleased with seeing any material thing, nor the ear with hearing. Study, therefore, to withdraw the love of your soul from all things that are visible, and to turn it to things that are invisible. Those who follow their own sensuality hurt their own cause and lose the grace of God.

2. Against Vain, Secular Learning, and of a Humble Knowledge of Ourselves

Every man by nature desires to know, but of what avail is knowledge without the fear of God? A humble farm laborer who serves God is more acceptable to Him than an inquisitive philosopher who, considering the constellations of heaven, willfully forgets himself. He who knows himself well is mean and abject in his own sight, and takes no delight in the vain praise of men. If I knew all things in this world, but knew without charity, what would it avail me before God, who judges every man according to his deeds? Let us, therefore, cease from the desire of such vain knowledge, for often great distraction and the deceit of the enemy are found in it, and so the soul is much hindered and blocked from the perfect and true love of God.

Those who have great learning desire generally to seem to be accounted wise in the world. But there are many things whose knowledge brings but little profit and little fruit to the soul; he is most unwise who gives heed to any other thing except what will profit him to the health of his soul. Words do not feed the soul, but a good life refreshes the mind, and a clean conscience brings a man to a firm and stable trust in God. The more knowledge you have, the more grievously will you be judged for its misuse, if you do not live according to it. Therefore, do not lift yourself up into pride, because of any skill or knowledge that is given you, but have the more fear and dread in your heart—for it is certain that, hereafter, you must yield a stricter accounting. If you think that you know many things and have great learning, then know for certain that there are many more things you do not know. So with true wisdom you may not think yourself learned, but ought rather to confess your ignorance and folly. Why will you prefer yourself in knowledge before another, since there are many others more excellent and more wise than you and better learned in the Law? If you would learn anything and know it profitably to the health of your soul, learn to be unknown and be glad to be considered despicable and as nothing.

The highest and most profitable learning is this: that a man have a truthful knowledge and a full despising of himself. More, not to presume of himself, but always to judge and think well and blessedly of another, is a sign and token of great wisdom and of great perfection and of singular grace. If you see any person sin or commit any great crime openly before you, do not judge yourself to be better than he, for you know not how long you shall persevere in goodness. We are all frail, but you shall judge no man more frail than yourself.

3. *Of the Teaching of Truth*

Happy and blessed is he whom truth teaches and informs, not by symbols and deceitful voices, but as the truth is. Our opinion, our intelligence, and our understanding often deceive us, for we do not see the truth. Of what use is the knowledge of such things as will neither help us on the day of judgment if we know them, nor hurt us if we do not know them? It is, therefore, great folly to be negligent of such things as are profitable and necessary to us, and to labor for such things as are worthless and to be condemned. Truly, if we so act, we have eyes but see not.

And of what avail is knowledge of the variety and operations of creatures? Truly, nothing. He to whom the everlasting Word, that is, Jesus, speaks, is freed of many vain opinions. From that Word all things proceed and all things openly show and cry that He is God. Without Him, no man understands the truth, or judges rightly. But a person to whom all things are one, and he who draws all things into one and establishes all things in one and desires nothing but one, may quickly be made firm in heart and fully at peace in God.

O Truth that is God, make us one with You in perfect charity, for all that I read, hear, or see without You is grievous to me; in You is all that I will or can desire! Let all learned ones be quiet in Your presence and let all creatures keep themselves in silence and do You only, Lord, speak to my soul. The more a man is one with You, and the more he is gathered together in You, the more he understands without labor high secret mysteries, for he has received from above the light of understanding. A clean, pure and constant heart is not broken or easily overcome by spiritual labors, for he does all things to the honor of God, because he is clearly mortified to himself. Therefore, he desires to be free from following his own will. What hinders you more than your own affections not fully mortified to the will of the spirit? Truly, nothing more.

A good devout man so orders his outward business that it does not draw him to love of it; rather, he compels his business to be obedient to the will of the spirit and to the right judgment of reason. Who wages a stronger battle than he who labors to overcome himself? And it should be our daily desire to overcome ourselves, so that we may be made stronger in spirit and go daily from better to better. Every perfection in this life has some imperfection attached to it, and there is no knowledge in this world that is not mixed with some blindness or ignorance. Therefore, a humble knowledge of ourselves is a surer way to God than is the search for depth of learning.

Well-ordered learning is not to be belittled, for it is good and comes from God, but a clean conscience and a virtuous life are much better and more to be desired. Because some men study to have learning rather than to live well, they err many times, and bring forth little good fruit or none. Oh, if they would be as busy to avoid sin and plant virtues in their souls as they are to dispute questions, there would not be so many evil things seen in the world, or so much evil example given to the people, or so much dissolute living in religion. On the day of judgment we will not be asked what we have read, but what we have done; not how well we have discoursed, but how religiously we have lived.

Tell me, where now are all the great students and famous scholars whom you have known? When alive, they flourished greatly in their learning, but now, others have succeeded to their posts and promotions, and I cannot tell whether their successors give them a thought. In their lifetime they were considered great in the world; now, little is spoken of them. Oh, how swiftly the glory of this world, with all its false, deceitful pleasures, passes away. Would to God their life had accorded well with their learning, for then would they have studied and read well. How many perish daily in this world by vain learning who care little for a good life and for the service of God. And because they desire to be great in the world rather than to be humble, they vanish away in their learning as smoke in the air.

He is truly great who has great charity. And he is great who is little in his own sight and who sets at naught all worldly honor. And he is very wise who accounts all worldly pleasures as vile dung, so that he may win Christ. And he is very well taught who forsakes his own will and follows the will of God.

4. That Easy Credence Is Not to be Given to Words

It is not good, truly, to believe every word or impression that comes; they ought to be pondered and considered advisedly and leisurely, so that Almighty God may not be offended through our fickleness. But alas, for sorrow, we are so frail that we quickly believe evil of others sooner than good. Nevertheless, perfect men are not so ready to give credence, for they well know that the frailty of man is more prone to evil than to good, and that he is very unstable in words. It is great wisdom, therefore, not to be hasty in our deeds, not to trust much in our own wits, not readily to believe every tale, not to show straightway to others all that we hear or believe.

Always take counsel of a wise man, and desire to be instructed and governed by others rather than to follow your own ingenuity. A good life makes a man wise toward God and instructs him in many things a sinful man will never feel or know. The more humble a man is in himself and the more obedient he is to God, the more wise and peaceful will he be in everything he will have to do.

5. On the Reading of Holy Scripture

Charity and not eloquence is to be sought in Holy Scripture, and it should be read in the same spirit with which it was first made. We ought also to seek in Holy Scripture spiritual profit rather than elegance of style, and to read simple and devout books as gladly as books of high learning and wisdom. Do not let the authority of the author irk you, whether he be of great learning or little, but let the love of every pure truth stir you to read. Ask not: Who said this; but heed well what is said. Men pass lightly away, but the truth of God endures forever.

Almighty God speaks to us in His Scriptures in various manners, without regard for persons, but our curiosity often hinders us in reading Scripture when we reason and argue things we should humbly and simply pass over. If you will profit by reading Scripture, read humbly, simply, and faithfully, and never desire to gain by your reading the name of learned. Ask gladly and heed humbly the sayings of saints, and do not disdain the parables of the ancient Fathers, for they were not spoken without great cause.

6. Of Inordinate Affections

When a man desires anything inordinately, he is at once unquiet in himself. The proud and covetous man never has rest, but the humble man and the poor in spirit lives in great abundance of rest and peace. A man not mortified to himself is easily tempted and overcome by little and small temptations. And he who is weak in spirit and is yet somewhat carnal and inclined to worldly things can with difficulty withdraw himself from worldly desires; when he does withdraw himself from them, he often has great grief and heaviness of heart and rebels if any man resists him. And if he obtains what he desires, he is disquieted by remorse of conscience, for he has followed his passion which has not helped at all in winning the peace he desired. By resisting passion, and not by following it, the truest peace of heart is won. There is, therefore, no peace in the heart of a carnal man or in the heart of a man who gives himself all to outward things. But in the heart of spiritual men and women who have their delight in God great peace and inward quiet are found.

7. That Vain Hope and Elation of Mind Are to be Fled and Avoided

He is vain who puts his trust in man or in any created thing. Be not ashamed to serve others for the love of Jesus Christ, and to be poor in this world for His sake. Trust not in yourself, but set all your trust in God: do all in your power to please Him and He will well assist your good will. Trust not in your own wisdom or in the wisdom or plans of any living creature, but instead, in the grace of God who helps humble persons and allows those who presume of themselves to fall until they are humbled. Glory not in your riches, or in your worldly friends, because they are mighty; let all your glory be in God only, who gives all things and desires to give Himself above all things.

Exult not in the strength or fairness of your body, for

by a little sickness it may soon be disfigured. Rejoice not in your ability or readiness of wit, lest you displease God, of whose free gift comes all that you have. Do not think yourself better than others, lest perhaps you be thereby belittled in the sight of God who knows all that is in man. Be not proud of your good deeds, for the judgments of God are different from the judgments of man, and what pleases man often displeases God. If you have any goodness or virtue, believe firmly that there is much more goodness and virtue in others, so that you may always keep yourself in humility. No harm comes if you hold yourself worse than any other, though it may not in truth be so, but much harm results if you prefer yourself above any other, even if he is ever so great a sinner. Great peace is with the humble man, but in the heart of a proud man are always envy and anger.

8. *That Much Familiarity Is to be Avoided*

Open not your heart to every person, but only to him who is wise, discreet, and reverent. Go seldom among strangers; neither flatter the rich nor bear yourself as an equal among the great. Keep company with the humble and the simple in heart, who are devout and of good deportment, and treat with them of things that may edify and strengthen your soul. Be not familiar with any woman, but commend all good women to God. Desire to be familiar only with God and with His angels; have a care to avoid the familiarity of man as much as you can. Charity is to be had toward all; familiarity is not expedient.

Sometimes it happens that an unknown person, whose good reputation commended him much, does not appeal to us when afterwards we meet him. We think sometimes to please others by our presence, but we displease them instead by all the evil manners and evil conditions they see and will consider in us.

9. Of Humble Subjection and Obedience and That We Should Gladly Follow the Counsel of Others

It is a great thing to be obedient, to live under authority and to seek our own liberty in nothing. It is a much surer way to stand in the state of obedience than in the state of authority. Many are under obedience more out of necessity than of charity and they have great pain and easily murmur and complain; they will never have liberty or freedom of spirit until they submit themselves wholly to their superiors. Go here and there where you will, you will never find perfect rest, save in humble obedience, under the governance of your proper superior. Dreaming of a change of place has deceived many a person in religion.

It is certainly true that many a person in religion is disposed to act after his own will and can agree best with those who follow his own ways, but, if we desire that God be among us, we must sometimes set aside our own will (though it seem good) so that we may have love and peace with others. Who is so wise that he can fully know all things? No one, surely. Therefore, trust not too much in your own judgment, but gladly hear the advice of others. And if, perhaps, the thing you would have done might be good and profitable, and yet you set aside your own will with regard to it and follow another's will, you will thereby find much profit. I have often said that to hear and take counsel is a more sure way than to give it. It is good to hear every man's counsel; not to agree with it, when reason demands agreement, is a sign of a great isolation of mind and of much inward pride.

10. *That We Should Avoid Superfluity of Words and the Company of Worldly-Living Persons*

Flee the company of worldly-living persons as much as you can, for the treating of worldly matters greatly hinders the fervor of spirit, even though it be done with a good intention. We are soon deceived by the vanity of the world and in a manner are made a slave to it, unless we take good heed.

I would I had held my peace many times when I spoke and that I had not been so much among worldly company as I have been. But why are we so glad to speak and commune together, since we so seldom depart without some harm to our conscience? This is the cause: By communing together we think to comfort each other and to refresh our hearts when we are troubled by vain imaginations, and we speak most gladly of such things as we most love, or else of things that are most irksome to us. But alas, for sorrow, all we do is vain, for this outward comfort is no little hindrance to the true inward comfort that comes from God.

It is necessary, therefore, that we watch and pray that time does not pass away from us in idleness. If it is lawful and expedient, speak, then, of God and of such things as are edifying to your soul and your neighbor's. Bad habits and neglect of our spiritual profit often make us take little heed how we should speak. Nevertheless, a devout communing on spiritual things sometimes greatly helps the health of the soul, especially when men of one mind and spirit in God meet and speak and commune together.

11. The Means to Get Peace, and of Desire to Profit in Virtues

We might have much peace if we would not meddle with other men's sayings and doings that do not concern us. How can he long live in peace who willfully meddles with other men's business and who seeks occasions for it straightway in the world and seldom or never gathers himself together in God? Blessed be the true, simple, and humble people, for they shall have a great plentitude of peace.

Why have many saints been so perfectly contemplative? Because they studied always to mortify themselves from worldly desires, that they might freely, with all the power of their heart, tend to our Lord. But we are occupied with our passions and are much busied with transitory things, and it is very seldom that we may fully overcome any one vice. And we are not at all quick to the performance of our duties, so we remain cold and slow to devotion. If we were perfectly mortified to the flesh and to the world, and were inwardly purified in soul, we should soon have a taste for heavenly things, and should to some degree experience heavenly contemplation. The greatest hindrance to heavenly contemplation is that we are not yet clearly delivered from all passions and concupiscence. We do not force ourselves to follow the way that holy saints have taken before us, but when any little adversity comes to us, we are at once cast down, and turn all too soon to seek human comfort. But if, like strong men and mighty champions, we would fight strongly in this spiritual battle, we should undoubtedly see the help of God come in our need, for He is always ready to help all who trust in Him. And He brings about occasions for such battles so that we may overcome and win the victory, and in the end have the greater reward.

If we place the end and perfection of our religion in outward observances, our devotion will soon be ended; and so we must set our axe deep to the root of the tree, so that, purged from all passion, we may have a quiet mind. If we would every year overcome one vice, we should soon come to perfection; but I fear rather, to the contrary, that we were better and more pure at the beginning of our conversion than we were many years after we were converted. Our fervor and desire for virtue should daily increase in us as we increase in age, but it is now thought a great thing if we may hold a little spark of the fervor that we had first. If we would at the beginning break the evil inclination we have to ourselves and to our own will, we should afterwards do virtuous works easily.

It is a hard thing to leave evil customs and it is harder to break our own will, but it is most hard forever to lie in pain and forever to lose the joys of heaven. If you do not overcome small and light things, how shall you then overcome the greater? Resist quickly at the beginning your evil inclinations and leave off wholly all your evil customs, lest, perhaps, by little and little they afterwards bring you greater difficulty. Oh, if you would consider how great inward peace you would have yourself, and how great gladness you would cause in others by behaving yourself well, I truly believe you would be much more diligent to profit in virtue than you have been before this.

12. Of the Profit of Adversity

It is good that we sometimes have griefs and adversities, for they drive a man to behold himself and to see that he is here but as in exile, and to learn thereby that he ought not put his trust in any worldly thing. It also is good that we sometimes suffer contradiction, and that we be thought of by others as evil and wretched and sinful, though we do well and intend well; such things help us to humility, and mightily defend us from vainglory and pride. We take God better to be our judge and witness when we are outwardly despised in the world and the world does not judge well of us. Therefore, a man ought to establish himself so fully in God that, whatever adversity befall him, he will not need to seek any outward comfort.

When a good man is troubled or tempted, or is disquieted by evil thoughts, then he understands and knows that God is most necessary to him, and that he may do nothing that is good without God. Then the good man sorrows and weeps and prays because of the miseries he rightly suffers. Then the wretchedness of this life burdens him, too, and he yearns to be dissolved from this body of death and to be with Christ, for he sees that there can be no full peace or perfect security here in this world.

13. Of Temptations to be Resisted

As long as we live in this world we cannot be fully without temptation, for, as Job says, the life of man upon earth is a warfare. Therefore, every man should be well on guard against his temptations, and watch in prayer so that his spiritual enemy, who never sleeps but always goes about seeking whom he may devour, may find no time or place to deceive him.

There is no man so perfect or so holy in this world that he does not sometimes have temptations, and we cannot be fully without them. Though they be for a time very grievous and painful, yet if they are resisted they are very profitable, for by them a man is made

44

more humble and is purified and instructed in various manners which he would never have known save through the experience of such temptations. All the blessed saints who are now crowned in heaven grew and profited by temptations and tribulations; those that could not well bear temptations, but were finally overcome, are held perpetual prisoners in hell.

There is no station so holy or any place so secret that it is fully without temptation, and there is no man fully free from it here in this life, for in our corruptible body we bear the matter whereby we are tempted, that is, our inordinate concupiscence with which we were born. As one temptation goes, another comes; and so we shall alway have something to suffer, and the reason is that we have lost our innocence.

Many people seek to flee temptation and fall the more deeply into it, for by merely fleeing we cannot win the victory, but by humility and patience we may be made stronger than all our enemies. He who merely flees the outward occasions and does not cut away the inordinate desires hidden inwardly in his heart shall gain little; temptation will easily come to him again and grieve him more than it did at first. Little by little, with patience and fortitude, and with the help of God, you will sooner overcome temptations than with your own strength and persistence. In your temptation it is good often to ask counsel. It is good not to be severe on any person who is tempted; rather, be glad to comfort him as you would be glad to be comforted.

The beginning of all evil temptations is inconstancy of mind and too little trust in God. As a ship without a rudder is driven hither and thither by every storm, so an unstable man who soon leaves his good purpose in God is variously tempted. Fire proves gold, and temptation proves the righteous man.

Many times we know not what we can bear, but temptation shows plainly what we are, and what virtue is in us. It is necessary at the beginning of every temptation to be well aware, for the enemy is soon overcome if he is not allowed to enter the heart, but is resisted and shut out as soon as he attempts to enter.

As medicine for the body is administered too late when the sickness has been allowed to increase by long continuance, so it is with temptation. First, an unclean thought comes to the mind, then follows a strong phantasm, then pleasure in it and various evil motions, and at the end follows a full consent; so, little by little, the enemy gains full entrance, because he was not wisely resisted at the beginning. The slower a man is in resisting, the weaker he is to resist, and the enemy is daily stronger against him.

Some people have their greatest temptation at the beginning of their conversion, some at the end, and some after a fashion are troubled with temptations all their life, and there are many who are but lightly tempted. And all this comes from the great wisdom and righteousness of God, who knows the state and merit of every person, and ordains all things for the best and for the everlasting health and salvation of His elect and chosen ones.

Therefore, we shall not despair when we are tempted, but shall the more fervently pray to God, that of His infinite goodness and fatherly pity He may vouchsafe to help us in every need; and that, according to the saying of St. Paul, He may so go before us with His grace in every temptation that we may be able to bear it. Let us, then, humble ourselves under the strong hand of Almighty God, for He will save and exalt all who are here meek and lowly in spirit.

In temptations and tribulations a man is proved, and how much he has gained is shown, and his merit is thereby the greater in the sight of God, and his virtues the more openly manifest. It is no great marvel if a man is fervent and devout when he feels no grief. But if he can suffer patiently in the time of temptation or other adversity and, despite it, stir himself also to fervor of spirit, it is a token that he will advance greatly thereafter in virtue and grace. Some people are kept from any great temptations, and yet are daily overcome in little and small occasions; that happens because the great goodness and patience of God would keep them in humility, so that they will not trust or presume of themselves, since they see themselves daily overcome so easily and in such little things.

14. That We Will Not Too Easily Judge Other Men's Deeds, or Cling Much to Our Own Will

Always have a good eye to yourself, and be careful not to judge other men too easily. In judging others a man often labors in vain, often errs, and carelessly offends God, but in judging himself and his own deeds he always labors fruitfully and to his spiritual profit. We often judge according to our own heart and affections, and not according to the truth. We lose true judgment through love of ourselves. But if God were always the whole intent of our desires, we should not so easily err in our judgments, or be so readily troubled because our own will has been resisted. But commonly there is in us some inward inclination or some outward affection which draws our heart along with them away from true judgment.

Many persons, through a secret love that they have for themselves, work indiscreetly according to their own will and not according to the will of God, yet they do not know it. They seem to stand in great inward peace when things go according to their own mind, but if anything happens contrary to their mind, they are soon moved with impatience and are quite downcast and melancholy.

From diversity of opinion dissension between friends and neighbors often springs, and also between religious and devout persons. An old habit is not easily broken, and no man will readily be moved from his own will; but if you cling more to your own will or to your own reason than to the humble obedience of Jesus Christ, it will be long before you are a man illumined by grace. Almighty God wills that we be perfectly subject and obedient to Him, and that we rise high above our own will and our own reason by a great burning love and a complete desire for Him.

15. Of Works Done in Charity

Not for anything in the world or for the love of any created thing is evil to be done. But sometimes, for the need and comfort of our neighbor, a good deed may be deferred or turned into another good deed. Thereby the good deed is not destroyed, but is changed into better.

The outward deed without charity is little to be praised, but whatever is done from charity, even if it be ever so little and worthless in the sight of the world, is very profitable before God, who judges all things according to the intent of the doer, not according to the greatness or worthiness of the deed. He does much who loves God much, and he does much who does his deed well, and he does his deed well who does it rather for the common good than for his own will. A deed sometimes seems to be done in charity and from a love of God, when it is really done out of worldly and fleshly love, rather than out of a love of charity. Commonly, some worldly inclination toward our friends, some inordinate love of ourselves, or some hope of a temporal reward or desire of some other gain moves us to do the deed, and not the pure love of charity.

Charity does not seek itself in what it does, but it desires to do only what will honor and praise God. Charity envies no man, for it loves no personal love.

Charity will not joy in itself, but desires above all things to be blessed in God. Charity knows well that no goodness begins originally from man, and therefore charity refers all goodness to God, from whom all things proceed, and in whom all the blessed saints rest in everlasting fruition. Oh, he who has a little spark of this perfect charity should feel in his soul with certain truth that all earthly things are full of vanity.

16. Of Bearing Other Men's Faults

Such faults as we cannot amend in ourselves or in others we must patiently suffer until our Lord of His goodness will dispose otherwise. And we shall think that perhaps it is best for the testing of our patience, without which our merits are but little to be considered. Nevertheless, you shall pray heartily that our Lord, of His great mercy and goodness, may vouchsafe to help us to bear such burdens patiently.

If you admonish any person once or twice, and he will not accept it, do not strive too much with him, but commit all to God, that His will may be done, and His honor acknowledged in all His servants, for by His goodness He can well turn evil into good. Study always to be patient in bearing other men's defects, for you have many in yourself that others suffer from you, and if you cannot make yourself be as you would, how may you then look to have another regulated in all things to suit your will?

We would gladly have others perfect, yet we will not amend our own faults. We desire others to be strictly corrected for their offenses, yet we will not be corrected. We dislike it that others have liberty, yet we will not be denied what we ask. We desire that others should be restrained according to the laws, yet we will in no way be restrained. And so it appears evident that we seldom judge our neighbors as we do ourselves.

If all men were perfect, what would we then have to put up with in our neighbors, for God's sake? Therefore, God has so ordained that each one of us shall learn to bear another's burden, for in this world no man is without fault, no man without burden, no man sufficient to himself, and no man wise enough of himself. And so it behooves each one of us to bear the burden of others, to comfort others, to help others, to counsel others, and to instruct and admonish others in all charity. The time of adversity shows who is of most virtue. Occasions do not make a man frail, but they do show openly what he is.

17. What Should Be the Life of a True Religious Person

It behooves you to break your own will in many things, if you would have peace and concord with others. It is no little thing to be in monasteries and in religious congregations, to continue there without complaining or speaking amiss, and faithfully to persevere there until the end. Blessed are they who there live well and come to a good end. If you would stand surely in grace, and profit much in virtue, consider yourself as an exile and a pilgrim here in this life, and be glad, for the love of God, to be considered in the world as a foolish and an unworthy person, as you are.

The religious habit and the tonsure help little; the changing of one's life and the mortifying of passions make a person perfectly and truly religious. He who seeks any other thing in religion than God alone and the salvation of his soul will find nothing there but trouble and sorrow; he will not remain there long in peace and quiet who does not labor to be the least, and subject to all.

It is good, therefore, to remember often that you came to religion to serve and not to be served, and that you are called in religion to suffer and to labor, and not to be idle or to tell vain tales. In religion, a person shall be proved as gold in a furnace, and no person in religion can remain long in grace and virtue unless he will humble himself with all his heart for the love of God.

18. *Of the Example of the Holy Fathers*

Behold the lively example of the holy fathers and blessed saints in whom flourished and shone all true perfection of life and all perfect religion, and you will see how little, almost nothing, we do nowadays in comparison with them.

Oh, what is our life when it is compared to theirs? They served our Lord in hunger and in thirst, in heat, in cold, in nakedness, in labor and in weariness, in vigils and fastings, in prayer and in holy meditations, in persecutions and in many reproofs.

Oh, how many and how grievous tribulations the apostles, martyrs, confessors, virgins, and other holy saints suffered who were willing to follow the steps of Christ. They refused honors and all bodily pleasures here in this life that they might have everlasting life. Oh, how strict and how abject a life the holy fathers in the wilderness led. How grievous the temptations they suffered, and how fiercely they were assailed by their spiritual enemies. How fervent the prayer they daily offered to God, what rigorous abstinence they kept. What great zeal and fervor they had for spiritual profit, how strong a battle they waged against all sin, and how pure and entire their purpose toward God in all their deeds!

In the day they labored and in the night they prayed,

and though they labored bodily in the day, they prayed in mind, and so they always spent their time fruitfully. They felt every hour short for the service of God, and because of the great sweetness they had in heavenly contemplation they often forgot their bodily nourishment. All riches, honor, dignity, kinsmen, and friends they renounced for the love of God. They desired to have nothing in the world, and scarcely would they take what was necessary for their bodily sustenance.

They were poor in worldly goods, but they were rich in grace and virtue; they were needy outwardly, but inwardly in their souls they were replenished with grace and spiritual comfort. To the world they were aliens and strangers, but to God they were dear and familiar friends. In the sight of the world and in their own sight they were vile and mean, but in the sight of God and of His saints they were precious and singularly elect. In them shone forth all perfection of virtue—true meekness, simple obedience, charity, and patience, with other similar virtues and gracious gifts of God; and so, they profited daily in spirit and obtained great grace from God. They are left as an example to all religious persons, and their lives should stir us to devotion, and to advance more and more in virtue and grace, than should the example of dissolute and idle persons hinder us in any way.

Oh, what fervor was in religious persons at the beginning of their religious lives, what devotion in prayer, what zeal for virtue, what love for spiritual discipline; and what reverence and humble obedience flourished in them under the rule of their superior. Truly, their deeds still bear witness that they, who so mightily subdued the world and thrust it under foot, were holy and perfect.

Nowadays he is accounted virtuous who is not an offender, and who may with patience keep some little spark of that virtue and of that fervor he had at first—but alas, for sorrow, it is through our own sloth and negligence, and through wasting our time, that we have so soon fallen from our first fervor into such a spiritual weakness and dullness that it is boring, as it were, to be alive. Would to God that the desire to profit in virtue were not so utterly asleep in us, who have so often seen the example of the blessed saints.

19. *Of the Exercises of a Good Religious Person*

The life of a good religious man should shine in all virtue and be inwardly as it appears outwardly. And it should be the much more inward, for Almighty God beholds the heart and we should always honor and reverence Him as if we were always in His bodily presence, and appear before Him as angels, clean and pure, shining with all virtue.

We ought every day to renew our purpose in God, and to stir our heart to fervor and devotion, as though it were the first day of our conversion. And we ought daily to pray and say: Help me, my Lord Jesus, that I may persevere in good purpose and in Your holy service unto my death, and that I may now today perfectly begin, for I have done nothing in time past.

According to our purpose and our intention shall be our reward, and though our intention be ever so good, it is necessary to bring to it a good will and great diligence. He who frequently proposes to do well and to profit in virtue nevertheless fails in the doing. What, then, shall another do, who seldom or never conceives such a purpose? Even if we intend to do the best we can, our good purpose may happen to be hindered in various ways; our special hindrance is that we carelessly abandon good exercises we used to engage in before. It is seldom seen that a good habit, willfully broken, may be taken up again without great spiritual hindrance. The purpose of righteous men depends on the grace of God more than on themselves and on their own wisdom. Man proposes, but God disposes. The way that a man shall walk in this world is found not in himself, but in the grace of God.

If a good habit is sometimes interrupted for the help of our neighbor, it may soon be taken up again, but if it be interrupted through sloth or negligence, it will hinder us greatly, and will with difficulty be taken up anew. Thus it appears that, though we encourage ourselves all that we can to do well, we shall easily fail in many things. Nevertheless, though we may not always fulfill it, it is good always to conceive such good purpose, especially against such things as impede us most.

We must also make diligent search, both within and without, to leave nothing inordinate unreformed in us, as fully as our frailty permits. And if you cannot do this continually, because of your frailty, at least see that you do it once in the day, evening or morning. In the morning you should make a good purpose for the day, and at night you should examine diligently how you have behaved yourself in word, in deed, and in thought, for in them we often offend God and our neighbor.

Arm yourself as Christ's true knight in humility and charity against all the malice of the enemy. Control gluttony and you shall the more easily control all carnal desires. Do not let the spiritual enemy find you idle, but take heed to be reading, writing, praying devoutly, meditating, or doing some other good labor for the common good. Bodily exercises are to be done in measure, for what is profitable to one is sometimes hurtful to another, and, spiritual labors done out of devotion are more surely done in private than in public.

And you must beware not to be more ready for private devotion than for those to which you are bound by the duty of your religious state. But when your duty is done, then add afterwards as your devotion will dictate. All may not use the same kind of exercise, but one person should use one kind and another person another, as each shall deem most profitable. Further, as the time requires, different exercises are to be used, for one kind of exercise is necessary on a holy day, another on an ordinary day. One kind is necessary in time of temptation, another in the time of peace and consolation; one kind when we have sweetness in our devotion, another when devotion grows cold. Moreover, at the time of principal feasts, we ought to be more diligent in good works than at other times. We ought to call devoutly for help to the blessed saints, who are then venerated in the Church of God, and to dispose ourselves precisely as if we were then about to be taken out of this world and brought to the everlasting feast of heaven. And since that bliss is yet withheld from us for a time, we may well think that we are not as yet ready or worthy to come to it, and so we ought to prepare ourselves to be more ready at another time. For, as St. Luke says: Blessed is that servant whom our Lord, when He shall come at the hour of death, shall find ready, for He shall take him and lift him up, high above all earthly things, into the everlasting joy and bliss of the kingdom of heaven.

20. *Of Love of Solitude and Silence*

Seek for a convenient time to search your own conscience, and think often of the benefits of God. Abandon curiosity and read such matters as shall stir you to compunction of heart for your sins, rather than only to pass the time. If you will withdraw yourself from superfluous words and from unprofitable business, and from hearing rumors and idle tales, you will find convenient time to be occupied in holy meditation.

The most holy men and women who ever lived fled, as far as they could, the company of worldly-minded men, and chose to serve God in the secret of their hearts. One holy man said: As often as I have been among worldly company, I have left it with less fervor of spirit than I had when I came. And this we well realize, whenever we talk long, for it is not so hard always to keep silence as it is not to exceed in words when we speak much. It is also easier to be always alone at home than to go forth into the world and not offend. Therefore, whoever intends to come to an inward fixing of his heart upon God and to have the grace of devotion must with our Saviour Christ withdraw from the world. No man can safely mingle among people save he who would gladly be solitary if he could. No man is secure in high position save he who would gladly be a subject. No man can firmly command save he who has learned gladly to obey. No man has true joy save he whose heart shows him to have a clean conscience. No man speaks surely save he who would gladly keep silence if he might.

The security of good and blessed men has always been in humility and in the fear of God. And though such good and blessed men shone in all virtue, they were not for that reason lifted up into pride, but were more diligent in the service of God and the more humble in all their doings. On the contrary, the security of evil men rises from pride and presumption, and in the end deceives them.

Therefore, do not think yourself secure in this life, whether you are a religious or a lay person. Frequently, those who have been esteemed in the sight of people as most perfect have been allowed to fall the more grievously because of their presumption. It is much more profitable, also, to many people that they sometimes have temptations than that they be always free from them, lest, perhaps, they think themselves all too secure, and so be lifted up into pride, or run to seek outward consolation.

Oh, how pure a conscience should he have who would despise all transitory joy and would never meddle with worldly business, and what peace and inward quiet should he have who would cut away from himself all busyness of mind, and think only on heavenly things.

No man is worthy to have spiritual comforts if he has not first been exercised in holy compunction, and if you will have compunction go into a secret place, and put aside all the clamorous noise of the world, for the prophet David says: Let the sorrow for your sins be done in your secret chamber. In your chamber you shall find great grace that you may lose easily outside. If your chamber is faithfully dwelt in, it will grow sweet and pleasant to you and will be a very dear friend for the future. But if it be indifferently dwelt in, it will grow very tedious and irksome. If in the beginning you are often in your chamber, and continue there in prayer and holy meditations, it will be afterward a most particular friend, and one of your most special comforts. In silence and quietness of heart a devout soul profits much and learns the hidden meaning of Scripture, and finds there many sweet tears of devotion as well, with which every night the soul washes itself mightily from all sin, that it may be the more familiar with God, to the degree that it is separated from the clamorous noise of worldly business. Therefore, our Lord and His angels will draw near and abide with those who, for the love of virtue, withdraw themselves from their acquaintances and from their worldly friends. It is better that a man be solitary and take good heed of himself than that, forgetting himself, he perform miracles in the world. It is also laudable in a religious person seldom to go abroad, seldom to see others, and seldom to be seen by others.

Why will you consider what it is not lawful for you to have? The world passes away with all its concupiscence and deceitful pleasures. Your sensual appetite moves you to go abroad, but when the time is past, what do you bring home but remorse of conscience and disquiet of heart? It is often seen that after a joyful going forth a mournful returning follows, and that a glad eventide causes a mournful morning. So all earthly joy begins pleasantly, but at the end it gnaws and kills.

What may you see outside your chamber that you may

not see within it? Look: Within your chamber you can see heaven and earth and all the elements of which all earthly things are made. And what can you see elsewhere under the sun that will long endure? And if you could see all earthly things, and have as well all bodily pleasures present at once before you, what would it be but a vain sight? Lift up your eyes, therefore, to God in heaven, and pray earnestly that you may obtain forgiveness for your offenses.

Leave vain things to those who would be vain, and take heed only of those things that our Lord commanded. Shut fast the door of your soul—that is to say, your imagination—and keep it cautiously, as much as you can, from beholding any earthly thing, and then lift up your mind to your Lord, Jesus; open your heart faithfully to Him, and abide with Him in your chamber, for you shall not find so much peace outside.

If you had not gone forth as much as you have, and had not given ear to idle tales, you would be in much more inward peace than you are. But because you took delight in hearing gossip and novelty, you shall suffer sometimes both trouble of heart and disquiet of mind.

21. Of Compunction of Heart

If you will find profit for the health of your soul, keep yourself always in the fear of God. Never desire to be completely at liberty, but hold yourself always under some wholesome discipline. As far as your weakness may bear it, never give yourself to indiscreet mirth for any reason. Have perfect compunction and sorrow for your sins, and you will find thereby great inward devotion. Compunction opens to the sight of the soul many good things which frivolity of heart and idle mirth soon drive away. It is a marvel how any man can be merry in this life if he considers well how far he is in exile out of his own country, and in how great peril his soul stands daily. But because of frivolity of heart and carelessness, we do not feel and we will not feel the sorrow of our own soul, and oftentimes we laugh when we ought rather to mourn, for there is no perfect liberty or true joy except in the fear of God, and in a good conscience.

That person is truly happy who has grace to avoid all things that hinder him from beholding his own sin; he is truly happy who can turn himself to God by inward compunction, and he is happy who also avoids all things that can offend or grieve his conscience. Fight strongly, therefore, against all sin, and fear not too much even though you are encumbered by a bad habit, for that bad habit can be overcome by a good habit. And do not make the excuse that you are impeded by other men; if you will abandon your familiarity with others, they will permit you to do your good deeds without hindrance. It is more expedient and more profitable that a man sometimes lack consolations in his life than that he always have them according to his own will, especially if they are earthly consolations. Nevertheless, it is our own fault that we sometimes do not have heavenly comfort, or that we so seldom feel such comfort. We do not seek to have true compunction of heart nor cast false outward comfort completely away. Consider yourself therefore unworthy to have any consolation and worthy to have much tribulation.

When a man has perfect sorrow for his sins, all worldly comforts are painful to him. A good man always finds matter enough over which he ought rightfully to sorrow, for, if he beholds himself, or if he thinks about his neighbor, he will see that no one lives here without great misery. And the more thoroughly he considers himself, the more sorrow he has, for the matter of true sorrow and of true inward compunction is always the remembrance of our sins, which surround us so completely that we can seldom appreciate spiritual things. But if we would more often think about our death than we do about long life, no doubt we should more fervently apply ourselves to our amendment. I believe also that, if we would heartily remember the pains of hell and of purgatory, we should more gladly bear all labors and sorrows, and that we should not dread any pain in this world, if by it we might avoid the pains that are to come. But since these things do not touch our hearts, and we still love the flattery and false pleasures of this world, we therefore remain cold and devoid of devotion. And oftentimes it is because of the weakness of the spirit that the wretched body complains so thoughtlessly.

Pray, therefore, humbly to our Lord that He of His great goodness give you the spirit of compunction, and pray with the prophet: Feed me, Lord, with the bread of compunction, and give me water of tears to drink in great abundance.

22. Of Considering the Misery of Mankind, and Wherein the Happiness of Man Abides

You are wretched wherever you are and wherever you turn, if you do not turn to God. Why are you so easily troubled? Because things do not happen to you as you desire. Who is the man who has all things as he would have them? Neither you nor I nor any man living, for no one lives in this world without some trouble or anguish, be he king or pope.

Who, in your opinion, is most in favor with God? Truly, he who gladly suffers most for God. But many persons weak and feeble in spirit pray in their hearts: See how good a life such and such a man leads. See how rich he is, how mighty, how high in authority, how great in the sight of the people, and how fair and how beautiful in appearance! If you will give heed to everlasting goodness, you will see that these worldly possessions and desires are of little worth, and that they are rather more irksome than pleasant, for they cannot be had or kept except by great labor and busyness of mind. The happiness of man does not depend on an abundance of worldly goods, because moderation is best.

And truly, to live in this world is but misery, and the more spiritual a man would be the more painful is it to him to live, and the more plainly he feels the defects of man's corruption. To eat, to drink, to sleep, to wake, to rest, to labor, and to serve all other needs of the body is great misery and great affliction to a devout soul, who would gladly be free from the bondage of sin, so that he might without hindrance serve our Lord in purity of conscience and in cleanness of heart. The recollected man is greatly grieved because of the necessities of his body in this world, and so the prophet David desired to be delivered from such necessities; but woe to those who do not know their own misery and woe to those who love this wretched and corruptible life. Some love it so much that, if they might live here forever, though they would earn their living but poorly with labor and begging, they would never care for the kingdom of heaven. Oh, insane and unfaithful creatures are those who so deeply fix their love in earthly things that they have no feeling or taste except in fleshly pleasures. True, in the hour of death they will know how mean and worthless were the things they so much loved. But the saints and devout followers of Christ gave no heed to what pleased the flesh, or to what was pleasant in the sight of the world. They fixed all their intention and desire on things invisible, and feared lest by sight of visible things they might be drawn down to love them.

My well-beloved brother, do not lose the desire to profit in spiritual things, for you have yet good time and space. Why will you put off the time any longer? Arise, and at this very moment begin and say: Now is time to labor in good works; now is time to fight the spiritual battle; now is time to make amends for past trespasses.

When you are troubled is the best time to merit and win reward from God.

It behooves you to go through fire and water before you can come to this point of reformation, but unless you have full mastery of yourself you will never overcome sin or live without great weariness and sorrow. We would gladly be delivered from all misery and sin, but because we have through sin lost our innocence, we have also lost joy and happiness, and so we must keep ourselves in patience, and with good hope await the mercy of God until wretchedness is past and this bodily life is changed into everlasting life.

Oh, how great is the frailty of man that is ever ready and prone to sin! Today you have confessed; tomorrow you fall again. Now you determine to take care, and you intend to go forward strongly in good works; shortly afterwards you act as though you had never taken such a resolution. Rightfully, therefore, we ought to humble ourselves, and never think that any virtue or goodness is in us, since we are so frail and so unstable. What was won with great difficulty, with much labor and special grace may soon be lost through negligence. Moreover, what shall become of us in the end, when we so swiftly grow dull and slow? Truly, sorrow and woe shall come to us, if we give into bodily rest now, as though we were in spiritual security, when there is as yet neither sign or token of virtue nor of good living in our manner of life. Wherefore, it would be of advantage to us if we were instructed again as novices to learn a good manner of life, if perhaps by that means there would be found in us hereafter any hope of amendment and spiritual profit in our way of living.

23. *Of the Remembrance of Death*

The hour of death will shortly come, and therefore take care how you conduct yourself, for the common proverb is true: Today a man; tomorrow none. When you are out of sight you are soon out of mind, and soon will be forgotten.

Oh, the great dullness and hardness of man's heart, which thinks only about present things and gives little care to the life to come. If you acted well, you should so behave in every deed and in every thought as though you were about to die this very instant. If you had a good conscience, you would not fear death so much, and it would be better for you to abandon sin than to fear death. Oh, my dear brother, if you are not ready this day, how will you be ready tomorrow? Tomorrow is a day uncertain, and you cannot tell whether you will live that long.

What profit is it to us to live long, if in a long life we so little amend our life? Long life does not always bring us to amendment; often, it brings an increase of sin. Would to God that we might one day be truly converted in this world! Many count up their years of conversion, yet but little fruit of amendment or of any good example is seen in their manner of life. If it is fearful to die, perhaps it is more perilous to live long. Blessed are those who have the hour of death ever before their eyes, and who every day prepare themselves to die.

If you ever saw any man die, remember that you must go the same way. In the morning, doubt whether you will live till night; at night, do not think yourself certain to live till morning. Be always ready, and live in such manner that death may not find you unprepared. Remember how many have died suddenly and unprepared, for our Lord called them in the hour they least suspected His summons.

And when this last hour comes, you will begin to feel quite differently than you did before about your past life, and you will begin to sorrow greatly that you were so slow and negligent in the service of God. Oh, how happy and wise, therefore, he is who labors to stand now in the condition in which he would like to be found at the moment of his death! Truly, a perfect despising of the world and a fervent desire to advance in virtue, a love to be taught, a fruitful labor in the works of penance, a ready will to obey, a complete forsaking of ourselves, and a willing bearing of all adversities for the love of God—all these shall give us a great trust that we shall die well.

Now while you are in good health you may do many good deeds; if you fall sick, I cannot tell what you may do, for few are made better through sickness, just as those who go on many pilgrimages are seldom made perfect and holy by them. Do not put your trust in your friends and neighbors, and do not put off your good deeds until after your death, for you shall be sooner forgotten than you think. It is better to provide for yourself ahead of time and to send some good deeds before you than to trust to others who very likely will easily forget you. If you are not busy now for yourself and for your own soul's health, who will be busy for you after your death? Now the time is very precious, but, alas, that you should spend so unprofitably the time with which you should win life everlasting! The time is to come when you will long for one day or one hour in which to make amends, but I do not know whether the day or hour will be granted to you. Oh, my dear brother, from how great peril and fear might you now deliver yourself, if you would always in this life fear to offend God, and always keep present before you the coming of death! Therefore, study so to live now that at the hour of death you may rejoice rather than fear. Learn now to die to the world so that you may then live with Christ. Learn also to despise now all worldly things so that you may then go freely to Christ. Chastise your body now with penance that you may then have a sure mind and a steadfast hope of salvation.

You are foolish if you think to live long, since you are not certain to live one day through to the end. How many have been deceived through trusting in a long life who have suddenly been taken out of the world much sooner than they had thought. How often have you heard that such a man was slain, and such a man was drowned, and such a man fell and broke his neck; this man choked on his food, and this man died in his recreation; one by fire, another by the sword, another by sickness, and some by theft have suddenly perished. And so the end of all men is death, and the life of man is as a shadow which suddenly glides and passes away. Think often who shall remember you after your death, and who shall pray for you, and do now for yourself all that you can, for you know not when you shall die, or what shall follow after your death. While you have time, gather to yourself immortal riches. Think unceasingly on nothing but on your soul's health. Devote your study only to things that are of God, and that belong to His honor. Make friends for yourself in readiness for that time. Worship His saints and follow their steps, so that when you go out of this world they may receive you into everlasting tabernacles.

Keep yourself as a pilgrim and a stranger here in this world, as one to whom the world's business counts but little. Keep your heart free, and always lift it up to God, for you have here no city long abiding. Send your desires and your prayers always up to God, and pray with perseverance that your soul at the hour of death may blessedly depart out of this world and go to Christ.

24. Of the Last Judgment, and of the Punishment Ordained for Sin

In all things behold your end, and often remember how you shall stand before the high Judge from whom nothing is hid. He will neither be pleased by favors nor countenance any kind of excuse, but in all things will judge as is just and true.

Oh, most unwise and most wretched sinner, what will you then answer to God, who knows all your sins and wretchedness, when you here sometimes dread the face of a mortal man? Why do you not now provide for yourself in preparation for that day, since you cannot then be excused or defended by another, for every man shall then have enough to do to answer for himself. But now your labor is fruitful, your weeping is acceptable, your mourning is worthy to be heard, and your sorrow also is a satisfaction for sin and washes it away.

The patient man who suffers injuries and wrong from others, yet sorrows more for their malice than for the wrong done to himself, has a wholesome and blessed purgatory in this world, and so have they who can gladly pray for their enemies and for those who oppose them, and those, too, who in their heart can forgive those who offend them, and those who do not wait long to ask forgiveness. And so do those have here a blessed purgatory who are more easily stirred to mercy than to vengeance and who can, as if by violence, break down their own will and strongly resist sin; and those, finally, who labor always to subdue their body to the spirit.

It is better to purge away sin now and to put away vice than to keep it to be purged away hereafter. Truly, we deceive ourselves by the inordinate love we have for our body's condition. What shall the fire of purgatory devour but your sin? Truly, nothing. Therefore, the more you spare yourself now and the more you follow your fleshly desires, the more grievously will you wail hereafter, and the more matter you save for the fire of purgatory.

A man will be most punished in the things in which he most offended. Slothful persons will in purgatory be pricked with burning prongs of iron, and gluttons will be tormented with great hunger and thirst. Lecherous persons and lovers of voluptuous pleasure will be filled with burning pitch and brimstone, and envious persons will wail and howl as mad dogs do. There will be no sin without its special torment. The proud man will be filled with shame and confusion, and the covetous man pinched with penury and need. One hour there in pain will be more grievous than a hundred years here in the sharpest penance. The souls of the damned will have no rest or consolation, but here we feel relief of our pain sometimes, and have consolation from our friends.

Be sorrowful for your sins now, so that at the day of judgment you may be happy with the blessed saints. Then a righteous man will stand in great constancy against those who have wronged him and oppressed him here. Then he will stand as a judge who here submits himself humbly to the judgment of men. Then the humble man will have great confidence and trust in God, and the obstinate, proud man will quake and dread. Then it will appear that he was wise in this world who, for the love of God, was content to be taken as a fool and to be despised and set at naught. Then he will be greatly pleased that he suffered patiently the tribulation of this world and all wickedness shall stop its mouth. Then every devout person will be joyful and glad, and the unreligious will weep and fear. Then the flesh that has been chastised with discretion will have more joy than if it had been nourished with all delight and pleasure. Then the poor garment will shine clear in the sight of God, and the precious raiment will grow foul and loathsome to the sight. Then the poor cottage will be more highly praised than the palace overgilded with gold. Then a steady patience will help more than all worldly power and riches. Then humble obedience will be exalted more highly than all worldly wisdom and policy, and a good clean conscience will then make us more glad and merry than knowledge of all philosophy. Then the despising of worldly goods will be of more worth than all worldly riches and treasure. Then you will have more comfort from your devout prayers than from all your delicate repasts. Then you will have more joy from silence than from long talking and gossiping. Then good deeds will be fully rewarded and fair words but little regarded. Then a strict life and hard penance will please more than all worldly delight and pleasure.

Learn now, accordingly, to suffer the small tribulations in this world so that you may then be delivered from the greater tribulations ordained in the other world for sin. First, put to the test here what you may suffer hereafter, and if now you cannot suffer even so little a pain, how will you then suffer everlasting torment—and if now even a little suffering makes you impatient, what will the fire of purgatory or, more, the fire of hell make you feel hereafter? You cannot have two heavens—that is to say, you cannot have joy and delight here, and also joy afterwards with Christ in heaven. Moreover, if you had lived always, to this present day, in honor and in sensual delight, what would it profit you now—if you should, at this present instant, depart from the world? Therefore, all is vanity but to love God and serve Him.

He who loves God with all his heart dreads neither death, torment, judgment, nor hell, for perfect love opens a sure passage to God. But if a man delights in sin, it is no marvel that he still dreads both death and hell, and though such a dread is only a servile fear, nevertheless it is good; for the fear of hell may withhold us from sin, if the love of God does not withdraw us from it.

He who ignores the fear of God cannot long stand in

the state of grace, but he will soon run into the snares of the devil and will easily be deceived by him.

25. *Of the Fervent Amending of All Our Life, and That We Especially Heed Our Own Soul's Health before All Else*

My son, be wakeful and diligent in the service of God, and think often of why you have come here, and why you have forsaken the world. Was it not that you should live for God, and be made a spiritual man? Yes, truly.

Therefore, stir yourself to perfection, for in a short time you will receive the full reward of all your labors, and from then on, sorrow and fear will never come to you. Your labor will be little and short, and you will receive in return everlasting labor and comfort. If you remain faithful and fervent in good deeds, without doubt our Lord will be faithful and liberal to you in His rewards. You will always have a deep trust that you will win the crown of victory, but you will not consider yourself certain of it, lest you grow slothful and proud of heart. A certain person who often doubted whether he was in the state of grace once fell prostrate in church and said: Oh, that I might know whether I shall persevere in virtue to the end of my life, and soon he heard inwardly in his soul the answer of our Lord, saying: What would you do now if you knew you should persevere? Do now as you would do then and you will be saved. And so at once he was comforted, and committed himself wholly to the will of God, and all his doubts ceased, and never after did he curiously search to know what should become of him, but he studied to know what the will of God was concerning him, and how he might begin and end all his deeds to the pleasure of God and to His honor. Trust in God, and do good deeds.

Inhabit the earth and you shall be fed with the riches of your good deeds, says the prophet David.

One thing withholds many from growing in virtue and from an amendment of life—and that is a horror and a false worldly fear that they may not be able to stand the pain and labor needed to win virtue. But they will profit most in virtue who force themselves vigorously to overcome those things that are most grievous and irksome to them. A man profits most and wins most grace in those things in which he has most overcome himself, and in which he has most subjected his body to his soul.

But not all men have in the same way much to mortify and overcome, for some have stronger passions than others. Nevertheless, a fervent lover of God, even if he has stronger passions, will yet be stronger to advance in virtue than another who is of better disposition and has fewer passions, but is less fervent toward virtue. Two things greatly help a man to amendment of life. They are a strong withdrawal of himself from those things to which his body most impels him, and a fervent labor for the virtues he most needs.

Study also to overcome in yourself those things that displease you most in others, and always gather some special profit from any place at all. For instance, if you see any good example, make yourself follow it, and if you see any evil example, see that you avoid it. As your eye considers the works of others, so and in the same manner your works are considered by others.

Oh, how joyous and how delightful it is to see religious men devout and fervent in the love of God, well mannered and well taught in spiritual knowledge; on the contrary, how oppressive and sorrowful it is to see them live inordinately, not making use of those things they have chosen and devoted themselves to. Also, how ill-befitting a thing it is that a man be negligent in the very purpose of his first calling, and set his mind on those things that are not allowed him.

Think often, therefore, on the purpose you have set

before you, and keep before the eye of your soul the intention of Christ's Passion. And if you behold well and lovingly His blessed life, you may well be ashamed that you have not better conformed your life to His. He who inwardly and devoutly exercises himself in the blessed life and Passion of our Lord Jesus Christ will find copiously therein all that is necessary for him, so that he will not need to seek anything apart from Christ. Oh, if Jesus Crucified were often in our hearts and in our memory, we should soon be learned in all things that are necessary for us.

A good religious man who is fervent in his life takes all things well and gladly does all that he is commanded to do. But a religious person who is negligent and slothful has trouble upon trouble and suffers great anguish and pain on every side, for he lacks true inward comfort, and is prohibited to seek outward comfort. Therefore, a religious person who lives without discipline is likely to fall to great ruin. He in religious life who seeks to have liberty and relaxation of his duty will always be in anguish and sorrow, for one thing or another will always displease him. Consider how other religious persons act who are strictly governed under the rules of their religious order. They seldom go forth; they live severely; they eat poorly, and are clothed roughly. They labor much, speak little, watch long, arise early, make long prayers, read frequently, and keep themselves always in some holy doctrine. Consider the Carthusians and the Cistercians, and many other monks and nuns of different orders—how they rise every night to serve our Lord. It would be a great shame to you, therefore, if you should grow slow and dull in so holy a work where so many glorify and praise our Lord.

Oh, how joyous a life it would be if we could do nothing else except continually praise our Lord with heart and mouth. Truly, if we could never need to eat, drink or sleep, but might always praise Him and take heed only to spiritual studies, then we would be much happier and blessed than we are now, when we are bound, of necessity, to serve the body. Oh, would to God that these bodily nourishments were now turned into spiritual food which, alas, we taste but seldom!

When a man comes to that point of perfection in which he seeks his consolation in no created thing, then God begins first to taste sweet to him, and then will such a man be content with anything that comes to him, whether he like it or not. And then he will not be glad for any worldly profit, however great it be, or pine because he lacks it, for he has set and established himself wholly in God, who is to him all in all. Nothing perishes or dies to God, but all things live to Him and serve Him without ceasing, after His command.

In everything remember your end, and remember that time lost cannot be called back again. Without labor and diligence you will never get virtue. If you begin to be negligent, you begin to be feeble and weak. But if you apply yourself with fervor, you will find great help from God, and to the love of virtue, you will find less pain in all your labors than you first did.

He who is fervent and loving is always quick and ready for everything that concerns God and His honor. It is greater labor to resist vices and passions than to toil and sweat in physical labor. He who will not flee small sins will, by little and little, fall into greater sins. You will always be glad at night when you have fruitfully spent the day before.

Take heed to yourself, and stir yourself always to devotion. Admonish yourself, and whatever you do for others, do not forget yourself. You will profit in virtue just so far as you can break your own will and follow the will of God.

BOOK II

Admonitions Leading to the Inner Life

1. *Of Inward Conversation*

The kingdom of God is within you, says Christ, our Saviour. Turn yourself, therefore, with all your heart to God, and forsake this wretched world, and you will soon find great inward rest. Learn to despise outward things, and give yourself to inward things, and you will see the kingdom of God come into your soul.

The kingdom of God is peace and joy in the Holy Spirit, such as is not granted to wicked people. Our Lord Jesus Christ will come to you and will show you His consolations, if you will make ready for Him a dwelling place within. All that He desires in you is within yourself, and there it is His pleasure to be. There are between Almighty God and a devout soul many spiritual visitings, sweet inward conversations, great gifts of grace, many consolations, much heavenly peace, and wondrous familiarity of the blessed presence of God.

Therefore, faithful soul, prepare your heart for Christ your Spouse, that He may come to you and dwell in you, for He Himself says: Whoever loves me will keep My commandments, and My Father and I and the Holy Spirit will make in him Our dwelling place.

Give to Christ, therefore, free entrance into your heart, and keep out all things that withstand His entrance. When you have Him, you are rich enough, and

He alone will be sufficient to you. Then He will be your provider and defender and your faithful helper in every necessity, so that you will not need to put your trust in any other save Him.

Man is soon changed, and easily falls away, but Christ abides forever, and stands strongly with His lover unto the end. No great trust is to be put in man, who is mortal and frail, though he be greatly profitable to you and much loved, nor is any great grief to be taken if he sometimes turns against you. Those who today may be with you, tomorrow may be against you; they often turn as the wind does.

Put your full trust, therefore, in God. Let Him be your love and fear above all things, and He will answer for you, and will do for you in all things as shall be most needful and most expedient for you. You have here no place of long abiding, for wherever you have come you are but a stranger and a pilgrim, and never will find perfect rest until you are fully joined to God. Why do you look to have rest here, since this is not your resting place? Your full rest must be in heavenly things, and you must behold all earthly things as transitory and shortly passing away. And beware well not to cling to them overmuch, lest you be seized with love of them, and so perish in the end.

Let your thought always be upward toward God, and direct your prayers continually to Christ. If you cannot, because of your frailty, always occupy your mind in contemplation of the Godhead, yet be occupied with a remembrance of His Passion, and make for yourself a dwelling place in His blessed wounds. And if you flee devoutly to the wound in Christ's side, and to the marks of His Passion, you will feel great comfort in every trouble. You will give little heed, even though you are openly despised in the world, and whatever evil word is spoken against you, will grieve you little.

Our Master Christ was despised by men in the world, and in His greatest need was forsaken by His acquaintances and friends, and left amid shame and rebuke. He was content to suffer wrongs, and to be set at naught by the world, and we desire that no person do us wrong, or belittle our deeds. Christ had many adversaries and revilers, and we would have all to be our friends and lovers. How can your patience be crowned in heaven, if no adversity should befall you on earth? If you would suffer no adversity, how can you be the friend of Christ? It behooves you to suffer with Christ, and for Christ, if you would reign with Christ.

Truly, if you had once entered the bloody wounds of Jesus, and had there tasted a little of His love, you would care nothing for the liking or the disliking of the world, but would rather have great joy when wrongs and injuries were done you, for perfect love of God makes a man perfectly to disregard himself. The true inward love of God that is free from all inordinate affections may soon turn freely to God, and in spirit lift itself up into contemplation, and fruitfully rest in Christ.

He who esteems all things as they are, and not as they are taken to be or thought to be by worldly people, is very wise, and is taught by God rather than by man. And he who can inwardly lift his mind up to God, and can regard outward things little, needs not to seek for time or place to pray, or to do other good deeds or virtuous works, for the spiritual man can soon recollect himself, and fix his mind on God, because he never allows it to be fully occupied in outward things. Therefore, his outward labors and his worldly occupations, which are necessary for the time, hinder him but little; as they come, he applies himself to them, and refers them always to the will of God. Moreover, a man who is well ordered in his soul heeds little the unkind and proud behavior of worldly people. As much as a man loves any worldly thing more than it should be loved, so much his mind is hindered from the true, ordered love he should have for God.

If you were well freed from all inordinate affections,

then whatever should befall you would turn to your spiritual profit, and to the great increase of grace and virtue in your soul. The reason why so many things displease and trouble you is that you are not yet perfectly dead to the world, or fully severed from the love of earthly things. And nothing so much defiles the soul as an unclean love for creatures.

If you cease to be comforted by worldly things, you may behold more perfectly heavenly things, and you shall then sing continually praise and blessing to God, with great joy and inward gladness. May the Holy Trinity grant this to you and me.

2. Of the Humble Acknowledgment of Our Own Defects

Do not regard much who is with you or who is against you, but let this be your greatest study: that God may be with you in everything that you do. Have a good conscience, and He will defend you well, and no evil will hinder or grieve the man God will help and defend. If you can be quiet and suffer for a while, you will, without doubt, see the help of God come in your need. He knows the time and place to deliver you, and therefore you must resign yourself wholly to Him. It is God's concern to help and to deliver from all confusion.

Nevertheless, it is often very profitable to us for the surer protection of humility that other men know our faults and rebuke us for them. When a man humbles himself for his offenses he easily pleases others, and reconciles himself to them whom he has offended. Almighty God defends and comforts the humble man; He inclines Himself to the humble, and sends him great plenty of His grace. God also shows His secrets to the humble man, and lovingly draws him to Himself, and after oppression He lifts him up to glory. When the humble man has suffered confusion and rebuke, he is in good peace, for he trusts God, and not the world. Moreover, if you will come to the height of perfection, do not think that you have advanced in virtue until you can feel humbly in your heart that you have less humility and less virtue than anyone else.

3. How Good It Is for a Man to be Peaceful

First put yourself at peace, and then you may the better make others be at peace. A peaceful and patient man is of more profit to himself and to others, too, than a learned man who has no peace. A man who is passionate often turns good into evil, and easily believes the worst. But a good, peaceful man turns all things to the best, and suspects no man.

He who is not content is often troubled with many suspicions, and is neither quiet himself nor allows others to be quiet. He often speaks what he should not, and fails to speak what it would be more expedient to say. He considers seriously what others are bound to do, but he grandly neglects that to which he himself is bound.

First, therefore, have a zealous regard to yourself and to your own soul, and then you may more righteously and with better ordered charity have zeal for your neighbor's soul. You are at once ready to excuse your own defects, but you will not hear the excuses of your brethren. Truly, it would be more charitable and more profitable to you to accuse yourself and excuse your brother, for, if you will be borne, bear with others. Consider how far you yet are from the perfect humility and charity of Christian people, who cannot be angry with any except themselves.

It is no great thing to get on well with good and docile men, for that is naturally pleasant to all people, and all men gladly have peace with those and most love

79

those who are agreeable. But to live peacefully with
evil men and with impertinent men who lack good manners and are illiterate and rub us the wrong way—that is
a great grace, and a manly deed, and much to be praised,
for it cannot be done save through great spiritual
strength. Some people can be quiet themselves, and live
quietly with others, and some cannot be quiet themselves, nor permit others to be quiet; they are grievous to
others—they are more grievous to themselves. And some
can keep themselves in good peace, and can also bring
others to live in peace. Nevertheless, all our peace,
while we are in this mortal life, rests more in the humble
endurance of troubles and of things that are irksome to
us than in not feeling them at all. For no man is here
without some trouble. Therefore, he who can suffer best
will have most peace, and he who is the true conqueror
of himself is the true lord of the world, the friend of
Christ, and the true inheritor of the kingdom of heaven.

4. *Of a Pure Mind and a Simple Intention*

Man is borne up from earthly things on two wings: simplicity and purity. Simplicity is in the intention; purity is
in the love. The good, true, and simple intention looks
toward God, and the pure love samples and tastes His
sweetness. If you will be free from inordinate love, no
good deed will prevent you from advancing by it in the
way of perfection. If you intend well, and seek nothing
but God and the profit of your own soul, you will have
great inward liberty of mind. And if your heart is
straight with God, then every creature will be to you a
mirror of life and a book of holy doctrine. No creature is
so little or so mean as not to show forth and represent
the goodness of God.

If you were pure and clean inwardly in your soul, then
you would without impediment take all things to the

best. A clean heart pierces both heaven and hell. What a man is inwardly in his conscience, that he shows himself to be by his outward deportment. If there is any true joy in this world, a man of clean conscience has it; if there is tribulation or anguish anywhere, an evil conscience knows it best. As iron put into the fire is cleansed from rust and is made all clean and pure, so, truly, a man who turns himself wholly to God is purged from sloth and is suddenly changed into a new man.

When a man begins to grow dull and slow in spiritual matters, then a little labor greatly frightens him, and he gladly seeks outward comfort from the world and the flesh. But when he begins perfectly to overcome himself and to walk strongly in the way of God, then he little considers those labors he before thought troublesome and insupportable.

5. Of the Knowledge of Ourselves

We may not trust much in ourselves or in our own intelligence, for often, through our presumption, we lack grace, and very little of the true light of understanding is in us. Many times we lose through our negligence what we have, yet we do not see, or want to see, how blind we are. Often we do evil, and in defending it do much worse, and sometimes, when we are moved by passion we think it zeal for God. We can quickly reprove small faults in our neighbors, but we do not see our own faults, which are much greater. We soon feel and deeply ponder on what we suffer from others, but we will not consider what others suffer from us. He who would well and righteously judge his own defects should not so rigorously judge the defects of his neighbors.

A man who is inwardly turned toward God takes heed of himself before all others, and he who can well take heed of himself can easily be quiet about other men's deeds. You will never be a spiritual man and a devout follower of Christ unless you can keep from meddling in other men's deeds and, especially, can give heed to your own deeds. If you will take heed wholly to God and to yourself, the faults you see in others will move you but little. Where are you when you are not present to yourself? And when you have run all about, and have considered other men's works, what has been your profit in it if you have forgotten yourself? So, if you will have peace in your soul, and be perfectly united to God in blessed love, set aside all other men's deeds, and set yourself and your own deeds only before the eye of your soul, and, if you see anything amiss in yourself, promptly reform it.

You will grow much in grace if you keep yourself free from all temporal cares, but if you set store by any temporal thing it will hinder you greatly. Therefore, let nothing in your sight be high, nothing great, nothing pleasing or acceptable to you, unless it be God alone, or things concerning God. Consider as vain all comforts that come to you from any creature. He who loves God and his own soul for God despises all other love, for He sees well that God alone is eternal and incomprehensible, and fills all things with His goodness, is the whole solace and comfort of the soul. He who loves God and his own soul for God sees that God is the very true gladness of our hearts, and no one else but only He.

6. *Of the Gladness of a Pure Conscience*

The glory of a good man is God's testimony that he has a good conscience. Therefore, have a good conscience, and you will always have joy. A good conscience can bear many wrongs and is constantly merry and glad in adversities, but an evil conscience is always fearful and unquiet. You will rest sweetly and blessedly if your own heart does not reprove you. Never be glad save when you have done well. Evil men never have perfect happiness, or feel inward peace, for our Lord says: There is no peace for wicked people. And though they say: We are in good peace, no evil thing shall come to us; lo, who can grieve or hurt us? do not believe them, for the wrath of God will fall suddenly upon them unless they amend, and all they have done will turn to naught, and whatever they should have done will remain undone.

It is not hard for a fervent lover of God to rejoice in tribulation, for all his joy and glory is in the Cross of our Lord Jesus Christ. Brief glory is what men can give, and, commonly, some grief follows after. The joy and gladness of good men is in their own conscience. The joy of righteous men is in God and of God, and their gladness is in virtue and in a good life. He who desires the very perfect joy that is everlasting puts little price on temporal joy, and he who seeks any worldly joy, and does not in his heart fully despise it, shows himself openly to love but little the joy of heaven.

He has great tranquility and peace of heart who does not regard praise or blame, and he will soon be at peace and content who has a good conscience. You are not the better because you are praised, or the worse because you are blamed, for as you are, you are, and whatever is said of you, you are no better than Almighty God, the Searcher of men's hearts, will testify that you are. If you behold well what you are inwardly, you will not care much what the world says of you outwardly. Man sees the face, but God beholds the heart; man beholds the deeds, but God beholds the intention of the deeds. It is a great sign of a humble heart that a man will do well, yet think that he has done but little; and it is a great sign of purity of life and of an inward trust in God when a man takes his comfort from no creature. When a man seeks no outward witness for himself, it appears that he has wholly committed himself to God. Also, as St. Paul says: He who commends himself is not justified, but he whom God commends. He who has his mind lifted up constantly to God and is not held by any inordinate affection is in the degree and in the state of a holy and blessed man.

7. *Of the Love of Jesus above All Things*

Blessed is he who knows how good it is to love Jesus and, for His sake, to despise himself. It behooves the lover of Jesus to forsake all other love besides Him, for He will be loved alone, above all others. The love of creatures is deceptive and disappointing, but the love of Jesus is faithful and always abiding. He who clings to any creature must of necessity fail as the creature fails. But he who cleaves abidingly to Jesus shall be made firm in Him forever.

Love Him, therefore, and hold Him for your friend, for, when all others forsake you, He will not forsake you, or suffer you finally to perish. You must, of necessity, leave your friends and the company of all men, whether you will or not, and therefore keep yourself in the company of your Lord Jesus, living and dying. Commit yourself to His fidelity, and He will be with you and help you when all others forsake you. Your Beloved is of such nature that He will not admit any other love, for He alone will have the love of your heart, and will sit therein as a king, on His proper throne. If you could empty yourself of the love of creatures, He would always abide with you and never forsake you.

You will find that all trust is, in a way, lost, which is put elsewhere save in Jesus. Do not, therefore, put your trust in anything that is only a reed full of wind, or a hollow stick which cannot hold you up or help you, but rather, when you need it most, will fail you. Man is but as grass, and all his glory is as a flower of the fields which suddenly vanishes away.

If you take heed only to the outward appearance you will soon be deceived, and if you seek your comfort in anything but in Jesus you will soon feel great spiritual loss. If you seek your Lord Jesus in all things you will truly find Him, but if you seek yourself you will find yourself, and that will be to your own great loss. Truly, a man is more grievous and more harmful to himself if he does not seek Christ than is all the world and all his adversaries together.

8. *Of the Familiar Friendship of Jesus*

When our Lord Jesus is present, all things are pleasing, and nothing seems hard to do for His love. But when He is absent, all things done for His love are painful and hard. When Jesus speaks not to the soul, there is no steadfast consolation. But if He speaks only one word, the soul feels great inward comfort. Did not Mary Magdalene soon rise from weeping when Martha showed her that her Master, Christ, was near and called her? Yes, truly. Oh, that is a happy hour when Jesus calls us from weeping to joy of spirit.

Remember how dry and how undevout you are without Jesus, and how unwise, how vain, and how ignorant you are when you desire anything but Jesus. Truly, such a desire is more harmful to you than if you had lost all the world. What can this world give you save through the help of Jesus? To be without Jesus is the pain of hell. And to be with Him is a pleasant paradise. If Jesus is with you no enemy can grieve you. He who finds Jesus finds a treasure, better than all other treasures, and he who loses Him has lost more than all the world. He is most poor who lives without Jesus, and he is most rich who is with Him. It is great wisdom to be closely familiar with Him and to keep Him. Be humble and peaceful, and Jesus will be with you; be devout and quiet, and He will abide with you.

You may soon drive your Lord Jesus away and lose His grace if you devote yourself to outward things. And if through negligence you lose Him, what friend will you then have? Without a friend you cannot long endure, and if Jesus is not your friend before all others you will be very downcast and desolate, and will be left without perfect friendship. And so you do not act wisely if you trust or take joy in any other thing besides Him. We should choose rather to have all the world against us than to offend God, and therefore, of all who are close and dear to you, let your Lord Jesus be the closest and dearest and more beloved than all others. And let all others be loved for Him, and He alone be loved for Himself.

Jesus is alone to be loved for Himself, for He alone is proved good and faithful beyond all other friends. In Him and for Him, enemies and friends alike are to be loved, and before all else we ought humbly and with diligence to pray to Him, that He may be loved and honored by all His creatures. Never crave to be singularly loved or commended, for that belongs only to God, who has none like Himself. And do not desire that anything occupy your heart, or that you be occupied with the love of any created thing, but that your Lord Jesus may be in you and in every good man and woman.

Be pure and clean within, free from the hindrance of any creature, as much as you can, for it behooves you to have a clean and pure heart toward Jesus if you will know and feel how sweet He is. Truly, you cannot come to that surety unless you are assisted and drawn through His grace and unless, all other things set aside, you are inwardly knit and joined to Him.

When the grace of God comes to a man, then he is made mighty and strong to do everything that belongs to virtue. And when grace withdraws, then a man becomes too weak and feeble to do any good deeds, and is as though he were left only to pain and punishment. If this happens to you, do not despair, and do not let good deeds go undone, but stand constant and firm, according to the will of God, and turn all things that happen to you to the praise and blessing of His Name. After winter comes summer. After the night comes the day. After the great storm clear and pleasant weather shines through again.

9. *Of the Lack of Solace and Comfort*

It is no great thing to despise the comfort of man when the comfort of God is present. But it is a great thing, and indeed a very great thing, that a man should be so strong in spirit as to bear the lack of both comforts, and for the love of God and for God's honor should have a ready will to bear desolation of spirit and yet in nothing to seek himself or his own merits.

What proof of virtue is it if a man is joyful and devout in God when grace comes and visits the soul—for that hour is desired by every creature. He rides quite safely whom the grace of God bears up and supports. And what marvel is it if he feel no burden, who is borne up by Him who is Almighty, and led by the sovereign Guide who is God Himself? We are always glad to have solace and consolation, but we desire to have no tribulation, and we will not easily cast forth from ourselves the false love of ourselves. The blessed martyr, St. Lawrence, through the love of God overcame mightily the love of the world and of himself. He despised all that was pleasant and delectable in the world, and humbly suffered Pope Sixtus, whom he loved most, to be taken from him; and so, through the love of God, he overcame the love of man, and instead of man's comfort he chose to follow the will of God. Do in like manner, and learn to forsake some necessary and some well-beloved friend for the love of God. Do not take it to heart when you are left or forsaken by your friend, for worldly friends must of necessity be separated. It behooves a man to fight long and mightily to strive with himself before he will learn fully to overcome himself and freely and readily to set all his desires in God. When a man loves himself much he soon inclines to man's comfort; but the true lover of Christ, and the diligent follower of virtue, inclines not so easily to comforts. He seeks little such sensible sweetness and bodily pleasure, and, instead, is glad to suffer great and hard pain and labor for the love of Christ.

Nevertheless, when spiritual comfort is sent to you by God, take it humbly and give thanks meekly for it. But know for certain that it is the great goodness of God that sends it to you, and not because you deserve it. See to it, then, that you are not lifted up to pride because of the comfort, and that you do not rejoice too much in it or presume vainly in it; instead, seek to be more humble for so noble a gift, and the more watchful and fearful in all your works. That time of comfort will pass away, and the time of temptation will follow shortly after.

When comfort is withdrawn, do not be cast down, but humbly and patiently await the visitation of God, for He is able and powerful to give you more grace and more spiritual comfort than you first had. Such alteration of grace is no new thing and no strange thing to those who have had experience in the way of God. Such alteration was found many times in the great saints and the holy prophets, and so the prophet David says: I have said in my abundance, I shall not be moved forever. That is to say, when David had abundance of spiritual comfort, he said to our Lord that he trusted he would never be deprived of such comfort. But afterwards, when grace withdrew itself, David said: You have withdrawn your face from me, and I am perturbed. That is to say: O Lord, You have withdrawn Your spiritual comfort from me, and I am left in great trouble and depression. Yet David did not despair because of this, but prayed heartily to our Lord and said: To You shall I cry, O

Lord, and I shall make petition to my God. That is, I shall busily cry to You, O Lord, and I shall humbly pray for Your grace and comfort. And soon he had the effect of his prayer, as he himself bears witness, saying: Our Lord has heard my prayer and has had mercy on me and has now again sent me spiritual help and comfort. And therefore he said afterwards: Lord, You have turned my joy into sorrow, and You have encompassed me about with heavenly gladness.

If Almighty God has thus acted with His holy saints, it is not for us weak and feeble persons to despair, though we sometimes have fervor of spirit, and are sometimes left cold and devoid of devotion. The Holy Spirit comes and goes after His good pleasure, and therefore Job says: Lord, You graciously visit Your lover in the morning (that is to say, in the time of comfort) and suddenly You prove him by withdrawing some comfort from him.

Wherein, then, may I trust, or in whom may I have any confidence, save in the great, endless grace and mercy of God? The company of good men and the fellowship of devout brethren and faithful friends, the possession of holy books or of devout treatises, the hearing of sweet songs or of devout hymns may avail little and bring but little comfort to the soul when we are left to our own frailty and poverty. And when we are so left, there is no better remedy than patience, with a complete resignation of our will to the will of God.

I never yet found any religious person so perfect that he did not experience at some times the absence of grace or some diminishing of fervor. And there was never yet any saint so highly exalted who did not, first or last, have some temptation. He is not worthy to have the high gift of contemplation who has not suffered some tribulation for God. The temptations preceding were a sure token of heavenly comfort coming afterwards, and great consolation is promised by our Lord to those who are found unshaken in their temptation. And therefore the Lord says: To him who overcometh I shall give to eat of the tree of life.

Heavenly comfort is sometimes given to a man so that he may be stronger to suffer adversity. But temptation follows so that he may not be lifted up into pride and think he is worthy of such consolations. The spiritual enemy does not sleep, and the flesh is not yet fully mortified, and therefore you must never cease to prepare yourself for spiritual battle, for you have enemies on every side who are ever ready to assail you and to hinder your good purpose all they can.

10. Of Yielding Thanks to God for His Many Graces

Why do you seek rest here, since you were born to labor? Dispose yourself to patience rather than to comfort, to bear the cross of penance rather than to have gladness. What man would not gladly have spiritual comforts, if he could always keep them? Spiritual comforts exceed by far all worldly delights and all bodily pleasures. All worldly delights are either foul or vain, but spiritual delights are only joyful and honest, brought forth by virtue, and sent by God into a pure soul. But no man can have such comforts when he would, for the time of temptation does not long delay.

The false liberty of will and the excessive trust we have in ourselves are quite contrary to heavenly visitation. Our Lord does well in sending such comforts, but we do not do well when we render no thanks to Him for them. The greatest reason why the gifts of grace do not easily come to us is that we are ungrateful to the Giver, and render no thanks to Him from whom all good things come. Grace is always given to those ready to give thanks for it, and therefore it is wont to be given to the humble man, and to be taken from the proud man.

I would have none of that consolation that should take compunction from me. I would have none of that contemplation that should lift my soul into presumption. Everything high in the sight of man is not holy; every desire is not clean and pure; every sweet thing is not good. All that is pleasant and dear to man is not always pleasant to God. We shall therefore gladly take such gifts as make us the more ready to forsake ourselves and our own will. He who knows the comforts that come through the gifts of grace and knows also how sharp and painful the absence of grace is will not dare think that any goodness comes from himself, but he will openly confess that of himself he is very poor and naked of all virtue. Give, therefore, to God what is His, and to yourself what is yours; that is, thank God for His manifold graces, and blame yourself for your offenses. Hold always in yourself a firm ground and a sure foundation of humility, and then the height of virtue will shortly be given to you, for the high tower of virtue cannot long stand unless it is based on the low foundation of humility.

Those who are greatest in heaven are least in their own sight, and the more glorious they are, the humbler they are in themselves, full of truth and heavenly joy, and not desirous of any vain glory or the praise of man. Also, those who are fully established and confirmed in God cannot in any way be lifted up into pride. They who ascribe all goodness to God seek no glory or vain praise in the world. They desire only to rejoice and to be glorified in God, and desire in heart that He may be honored and praised above all things, both in Himself and in His saints, and that is always what perfect men most desire to bring about.

Be loving and thankful to God for the least benefits that He gives you, and then you will be the better prepared and the more worthy to receive greater benefits from Him. Think that the least gift that He gives is great, and take the meanest things as special gifts and as great tokens of love. If the dignity of the Giver is well considered, no gift will seem little. It is no small thing that God gives, for, though He send pain and sorrow, we should take them gladly and thankfully, since all He permits to come to us is for our spiritual health. If a man desires to hold the grace of God, let him be affectionate and thankful for such grace as he has received, and patient when it is withdrawn. Let him pray devoutly that it may come again shortly, and then let him be meek and humble in spirit, so that he will not lose the grace through his presumption and pride of heart.

11. Of the Small Number of the Lovers of the Cross

Jesus has many lovers of His kingdom of heaven, but He has few bearers of His Cross. Many desire His consolation, but few desire His tribulation. He finds many comrades in eating and drinking, but He finds few who will be with Him in His abstinence and fasting. All men would joy with Christ, but few will suffer anything for Christ. Many follow Him to the breaking of His bread, for their bodily refreshment, but few will follow Him to drink a draft of the chalice of His Passion. Many honor His miracles, but few will follow the shame of His Cross and His other ignominies. Many love Jesus as long as no adversity befalls them, and can praise and bless Him whenever they receive any benefits from Him, but if Jesus withdraws a little from them and forsakes them a bit, they soon fall into some great grumbling or excessive dejection or into open despair.

But those who love Jesus purely for Himself, and not for their own profit or convenience, bless Him as heartily in temptation and tribulation and in all other adversities as they do in time of consolation. And if He never sent them consolation, they would still always bless and praise Him. Oh, how much more may the love of Jesus do for the help of a soul if it is pure and clean, not mixed with any inordinate love of itself! Therefore, may not they who always look for worldly comforts and for worldly consolations be called worldly merchants and worldly lovers rather than lovers of God? Do they not show openly by their deeds that they love themselves rather than God? Yes, truly. Oh, where may any be found who will serve God freely and purely, without looking for some reward in return? And where may any be found so spiritual that he is clearly delivered and freed from love of himself, truly poor in spirit, and wholly separated from love of creatures? I think none such can be found, unless it be far away in far countries.

If a man gives all his possessions for God, he yet is nothing, and if he does great penance for his sins, and if he has great wisdom and knowledge, he yet is far from virtue. And if he has great virtue and fervent devotion, he yet lacks much, and there is especially one thing most necessary to him. And what is that? It is that, forsaking all things and himself as well, he go clearly out of himself, and keep nothing to himself of any private love. And when he has done all that he ought to do, that he feel in himself as if he had done nothing, that he think little what some other one might think great, and that he believe himself, truly—as he is—an unprofitable servant. The Author of truth, our Saviour Christ, says: When you have done all that is commanded of you, yet say that you are but unprofitable servants. Then he who can do thus may well be called poor in spirit and stripped of private love, and he may well say with the prophet David: I am one with God, and poor and meek in heart. There is no one more rich, no one more free, no one more powerful than he who can forsake himself and all passing things and truly hold himself to be the lowest and meanest of all.

12. *Of the Way of the Cross, and How Profitable Is Patience in Adversity*

The words of our Saviour are thought very hard and grievous when He says: Forsake yourselves, take the Cross and follow Me. But it shall be much more grievous to hear these words at the Last Judgment: Go from Me, you cursed, into the fire that shall last forever. But those who now gladly hear and follow the words of Christ, by which He counsels them to follow Him, shall not then need to fear, hearing those words of everlasting damnation. The sign of the Cross shall appear in heaven when our Lord shall come to judge the world, and the servants of the Cross, who conformed themselves here in this life to Christ crucified on the Cross, shall go to Christ their judge with great faith and trust.

Why, then, do you dread to take His Cross, since it is the very way to the kingdom of heaven, and there is no other way? In the Cross is health, in the Cross is life; in the Cross is the fullness of heavenly sweetness; in the Cross is strength of mind, joy of spirit, height of virtue, full perfection of all holiness, and there is no help for the soul, or hope of everlasting life, save through the virtue of the Cross.

Take, therefore, your cross and follow Jesus, and you shall go to life everlasting. He has gone before you, bearing His Cross, and died for you upon that Cross so that you should in like manner bear with Him the cross of penance and tribulation, and that you should be ready in like manner for His love to suffer death, if need be, as He has done for you. If you die with Him you will live with Him; if you are His companion with Him in pain, you will be His companion in glory.

Behold, then, how in the Cross all things stand; and how, in dying to the world, lies all our health; and that there is no other way to life and true inward peace but the way of the Cross, and the way of daily submission of the body to the spirit. Go wherever you will, and reap whatever you desire, and you will never find, above you or beneath you, within you or without you, a more high, a more excellent, a more sure way to Christ than the way of the Holy Cross.

Arrange everything after your own will, and yet you will find that you must of necessity suffer something, either according to your will or against it, and so you will always find the Cross. You will either feel pain in your body or have trouble of spirit in your soul. You will be sometimes as if you were forsaken by God; sometimes you will be vexed with your neighbor and, what is yet more painful, you will sometimes be a burden to yourself. And you will find no means of deliverance save that it behooves you to suffer until it please Almighty God of His goodness to dispose otherwise for you. He desires that you should learn to suffer tribulation without consolation, so that you may learn to submit yourself wholly to Him, and by tribulation to be made more humble than you were at first. No man feels the Passion of Christ so efficaciously as he who feels pain like the pain Christ felt.

This Cross is always ready, and everywhere it awaits you, and you cannot flee it nor fully escape it, wherever you go. For, wherever you go, you will always bear yourself about with you, and so you will always find yourself. Turn where you will, above yourself and beneath yourself, within and without yourself, and you will find this Cross on every side, so that it will be necessary for you to keep yourself always in patience, and it behooves you to do this if you will have inward peace and deserve a perpetual crown in heaven.

If you will gladly bear this Cross, it will bear you, and it will bring you to the end you desire, where you will never afterwards have anything to suffer. But if you bear this Cross against your will, you make a great burden for yourself, and it will be the more grievous to you, and yet it behooves you to bear it. And if it happens that you put away one cross, that is to say, one tribulation, another surely will come, perhaps heavier than the first one was.

Do you hope to escape what no mortal man has ever yet escaped? What saint in this world has been without his cross and without some trouble? Truly, our Lord Jesus was not one hour without some sorrow and pain as long as He lived here. It behooved Him to suffer death and to rise again and so to enter into His glory. How is it, then, that you seek any other way to heaven than this plain, high way of the Cross. All the life of Christ was Cross and martyrdom; do you seek pleasure and joy? You err greatly if you seek any other thing than to suffer, for all this mortal life is full of misery and is all surrounded and marked with crosses. And the more highly a man profits in spirit, the more painful crosses will he find, for, by the firm certainty of Christ's love, in which he daily increases, the pain of this exile daily appears to him more and more.

Nevertheless, a man vexed with pain is not left wholly without all comfort, for he sees well that great fruit and high reward shall grow unto him by the bearing of his cross. And when a man freely submits himself to such tribulation, then all the burden of tribulation is suddenly turned into a great trust of heavenly solace. The more the flesh is punished by tribulation, the more the soul is daily strengthened by inward consolation. And sometimes the soul will feel such comforts in adversities, that for love and a desire to be conformed to Christ Crucified, it would not be without sorrow and trouble. The more it may suffer for His love here, the more acceptable it will be to him in the life to come. But this working is not in the power of man, save through the grace of God—that is to say, that a frail man should accept and love adversities that his natural inclinations so much abhor and flee.

It is not in the power of man gladly to bear the Cross, to love the Cross, to chastise the body and make it submissive to the will of the spirit, to flee honors gladly, to sustain reproofs, to despise himself and to desire to be despised, patiently to suffer adversities with all the displeasures that accompany them, and not to desire any manner of profit in this world. If you trust in yourself, you will never bring all this about. But if you trust in God, He will send you strength from heaven, and the world and the flesh will be made subject to you. Yes, and if you are strongly armed with faith, and are marked with the Cross of Christ as His family servant, you will not need to fear your spiritual enemy, for he will also be made subject to you, so that he will have no power against you. Steel yourself as a faithful servant of God manfully to bear the Cross of your Lord Jesus who, for your love, was crucified upon the Cross. Prepare yourself to suffer all manner of adversities and inconveniences in this wretched life, for so it will be with you wherever you hide yourself. There is no remedy for escaping, but you must always keep yourself in patience. If you desire to be a dear and well-beloved friend of Christ, drink effectively with Him a draft of the chalice of His tribulation. As for consolations, commit them to His will so that He may ordain them as He knows most expedient for you. But as for yourself, as much as lies in your power, dispose yourself to suffer, and when tribulations come, take them as special consolations, saying with the Apostle: The passions of this world are not worthy of themselves to bring us to the glory that is ordained for us in the life to come. And that is true, even though one man alone might suffer as much as all men together could suffer.

When you come to such a degree of patience that tribulation is sweet to you, and for the love of God is savory and pleasant in your sight, then may you trust that it is well with you, and that you are in good estate; for you have found paradise on earth. But as long as it

97

is irksome to you to suffer, and you seek to flee it, just so long it is not well with you, and just so long you are not in the perfect way of patience. If you could bring yourself to that disposition where you should be, that is, to suffer gladly for God and to die fully to the world, then it would shortly be better with you and you would find great peace.

Yet, although you were rapt with St. Paul into the third heaven, you would not therefore be secure and without all adversity. Our Saviour, speaking of St. Paul after he had been rapt into heaven, said: I shall show him how many things he shall suffer for Me. To suffer, therefore, remains your lot, if you will love your Lord Jesus, and serve without ceasing. Would to God you were worthy to suffer something for His love. Oh, how great joy it should be to you to suffer for Him, what gladness to all the saints in heaven, and how great edification to your neighbor. All men praise patience, yet few men will suffer. Rightly, then, should you suffer some small thing for God, who suffered much more for the world. After this bodily death you will still live, and the more you can die to yourself here, the more do you begin to live to God. No man is worthy to receive heavenly rewards unless he has first learned to bear adversities for the love of Christ. Nothing is more acceptable to God or more profitable to man in this world than to be glad to suffer for Christ, insomuch that, if it were given to your choice, you would choose adversity rather than prosperity, for then, by the patient suffering of adversity, you would be more like to Christ and the more conformed to all His saints. Our merit and our perfection in this life stand not in consolation and in sweetness, but in suffering great, grievous adversities and tribulations.

If there had been any nearer or better way for the health of man's soul than to suffer, our Lord Jesus would have showed it by word and by example. But because there was not, He openly exhorted His disciples who followed Him and all others who desire to follow Him to forsake their own will and to take the cross of penance and follow Him, saying: Whosoever will come after Me, let him forsake his own will, take the cross and follow Me. And so, when all things are searched and read, this is the final conclusion: By many tribulations it behooves us to enter into the kingdom of heaven, and may Our Lord Jesus Christ bring us there.

BOOK III

The Inward Speaking of Christ to a Faithful Soul

1. Of the Inward Speaking of Christ to a Faithful Soul

I shall take heed, says a devout soul, and I shall hear what my Lord Jesus will say to me.

Blessed is that man who hears Jesus speaking in his soul, and who takes from His mouth some word of comfort. Blessed are those ears which hear the secret whisperings of Jesus, and give no heed to the deceitful whisperings of this world, and blessed are the good plain ears which heed not outward speech but what God speaks and teaches inwardly in the soul. Blessed are those eyes which are shut to the sight of outward vanities and give heed to the inward movings of God. Blessed are they, too, who win virtue and prepare themselves by good bodily and spiritual works to receive daily more and more the secret inspirations and inward teachings of God. And blessed are they who set themselves wholly to serve God and who for His service put away all worldly hindrances.

O my soul, take heed to what has been said before and shut the doors of your sensuality, which are your five senses, so that you may hear inwardly what our Lord Jesus speaks within your soul. Thus says your beloved: I am your health, I am your peace, I am your life. Keep yourself in Me and you will find peace in Me. Forsake the love of transitory things and seek things that are ever-lasting. What are all temporal things but deceptive? And what help can any creature be to you if your Lord Jesus forsake you? Therefore, forsaking and leaving all creatures and all worldly things, do what lies in you to make yourself pleasing in His sight, so that you may after this life come to everlasting life in the kingdom of heaven.

2. How Almighty God Speaks Inwardly to Man's Soul without Sound of Words

Speak, Lord, for I, Your servant, am ready to hear You. I am Your servant: give me wisdom and understanding to know Your commandments. Bow my heart to follow Your holy teachings, that they may sink into my soul like dew into the grass. The children of Israel said to Moses: Speak to us and we will hear you, but let the Lord not speak to us, lest perhaps we die for dread. Not so, Lord, not so, I beseech You! Rather, I ask humbly with Samuel the prophet that you vouchsafe to speak to me Yourself, and I shall gladly hear You. Do not let Moses or any other of the prophets speak to me, but You Yourself, Lord, the inward inspirer and giver of light to all the prophets. You alone, without them, can fully inform and instruct me; they, without You, can profit me little.

They speak Your words, but they do not give the spirit to understand the words. They speak fair, but if You are silent, they do not kindle the heart. They show forth fair letters, but You interpret the sentence. They reveal great high mysteries, but You open the true understanding of them. They declare Your commandments, but You help to their performance. They show the way, but You give strength to walk in it. They do all outwardly, but You illuminate and instruct the heart within. They water only externally, but You give the inward growth.

They cry all in words, but You give to the hearers understanding of the words that are hard.

Do not let Moses speak to me, therefore, but You, my Lord Jesus, who are the everlasting Truth, lest perhaps I die and be made like a man without fruit, warmed from without, but not inflamed within, and so receive the harder judgment, because I have heard Your word and not done it, known it and not loved it, believed it and not fulfilled it. Speak, therefore, to me Yourself, for I, Your servant, am ready to hear You. You have the words of eternal life; speak them to me for the full comfort of my soul and give me amendment of all my past life, to Your joy, honor and glory, everlastingly.

3. That the Words of God Are to be Heard with Great Humility, and That There Are But Few Who Ponder Them as They Ought

My son, says our Lord, hear My words and follow them, for they are most sweet, far passing the wisdom and learning of all philosophers and all the wise men of the world. My words are spiritual and cannot be comprehended fully by man's intelligence. Neither are they to be adapted or applied according to the vain pleasure of the hearer, but are to be heard in silence, with great humility and reverence, with great inward affection of the heart and in great rest and quiet of body and soul.

Oh, blessed is he, Lord, whom You instruct and teach, so that You may be gentle and merciful to him on the evil day, that is, on the day of the most dreadful judgment, so that he will not then be left desolate and without comfort in the land of damnation.

Then our Lord answers: I have taught prophets from the beginning and I still do not cease to speak to every creature. But many are deaf and will not hear, and many hear the world more gladly than Me, and more easily follow the likings of the flesh than the pleasure of God.

The world promises temporal things of small value, yet is served with great affection; but God promises high and eternal things, and the hearts of the people are slow and dull. Oh, who serves and obeys God in all things with so great a desire as he serves and obeys the world, and as worldly princes are served and obeyed? I believe no one. Why? For a little benefit great journeys are undertaken, but for everlasting life people will scarcely lift their feet once from the ground. A thing that is of small price is many times busily sought, great contention sometimes rises over a penny, and for the promise of a little worldly gain men do not shrink to labor and sweat both night and day.

But alas, for sorrow! For everlasting goods, for the rewards that cannot be rightly valued by man's heart, for the high honor and glory that never shall have an end, men are slow to take any kind of pain or labor. Be ashamed, you slow servant of God, that they are found more ready for the works of death than you are for works of life, and that they rejoice more in vanity than you in truth. Yet, they are often deceived in that wherein they placed most trust, but My promise deceives no man nor does it leave without some comfort any man who trusts in Me. What I have promised I will perform, and what I have said I will fulfill to all persons, if they abide faithfully in My love, and fear to the end, for I am the rewarder of all good men and a strong tester of all devout souls.

Write My words diligently in your heart and often think on them; in time of temptation they will be most necessary to you. What you do not understand when you read you will understand at the time of My coming. I am wont to visit my servants in two kinds of ways: with temptation and with consolation. And two lessons I daily teach them: one whereby I rebuke them for their vices, the other whereby I stir them up to increase in virtue. He who knows My words but despises them stores up what will judge him on the last day.

A Prayer to Obtain the Grace of Devotion

O Lord Jesus, You are all my riches, and all that I have I have from You. But what am I, Lord, that I dare speak thus to You? I am your poorest servant, and a most abject worm, more poor and more despicable than I can dare to say. Behold, Lord, that I am nothing, that I have nothing, and that, of myself, I am worth nothing. You only are good, righteous, and holy. You put all things in order, You give all things, and You fill all things with Your goodness, leaving only the wretched sinner barren and devoid of heavenly comfort. Remember Your mercies and fill my heart with grace, for You do not will that Your works become in vain in me. How can I bear the miseries of this life unless Your grace and mercy comfort me? Turn not Your face from me, defer not to visit me. Do not withdraw Your comforts from me, lest, perhaps, my soul become as dry earth, without the water of grace and, as it were, a thing unprofitable to You. Teach me, Lord, to fulfill Your will, and to live humbly and worthily before You, for You are all my wisdom and learning. You are He who knows me as I am, and who knew me before the world was made, and before I was born or brought into this life.

4. How We Ought to be Conversant before God in Truth and Humility

My son, says our Lord Jesus, walk before Me in truth and humility, and seek Me always in simplicity and lowliness of heart. He who walks in truth will be defended from all perils and dangers, and Truth will deliver him from all deceivers and from all evil sayings of wicked people. If Truth deliver you, you are quite free, and you will care little for the vain sayings of people.

Lord, all You say is true. Be it done to me according to Your Word. I beseech You that Your truth may teach me, and keep me, and finally lead me to a blessed ending, and that it may deliver me from all evil affection, and from all inordinate love, so that I may walk with You in freedom of spirit and in liberty of heart.

Then the Truth responds to us: I shall teach you what is acceptable and pleasant to Me. Think on your past sins with great displeasure and sorrow of heart. Never think yourself worthy to be called holy or virtuous because of any good deeds you have done, but think how great a sinner you are, surrounded and hemmed in by manifold sins and passions, and that of yourself you revert to nothing, soon fall, soon are overcome, soon are troubled and broken by labor and pain. You have nothing for which you may properly extoll yourself, but many things for which you ought to despise yourself; for you are more unstable and weak in spiritual works than you know or think.

Let nothing, therefore, seem great to you, nothing precious, nothing worthy of good repute, nothing worthy to be praised in your sight, except what is eternal. Let the everlasting Truth be acceptable and most pleasant to you above all other things, and let your own sins and vileness be most unpleasant to you. Dread nothing so much, blame nothing so much, hate nothing so much, and flee from nothing so much as your sins and wickedness, for they should displease you more than the loss of all worldly things. There are some who do not walk purely before Me, because through pride and curiosity they desire of their own power to search and to know the high things of my Godhead, forgetting themselves and the health of their own souls. Such persons fall often into great temptation and into grievous sin because of their pride and curiosity, since I am turned against them, and leave them to themselves without My help or counsel.

Fear, therefore, the judgments of God and the wrath of Him who is Almighty, and do not discuss or search His secrets, but search well your own iniquities: how often and how seriously you have offended Him, and how many good deeds you have carelessly omitted and left undone, which you might well have done.

Some persons seek their devotion in books, some in images, some in outward symbols and figures; some have Me in their mouth, but little in their heart. There are some who have their reason clearly illuminated by the light of true understanding, and by it their affection is so purged and purified from earthly things that they always desire heavenly things, so that it is hard for them to hear of earthly things and a truly great pain to serve the necessities of the body, and they think all the time lost which is devoted to them. Such persons feel and know well what the spirit of Truth speaks in their souls, for it teaches them to despise earthly things and to love heavenly things, to forsake the world that is transitory, and to desire both day and night to arrive at last where joy is everlasting. May our Lord Jesus Christ bring us there.

5. *Of the Marvelous Effect of the Love of God*

Blessed may You be, heavenly Father, the Father of my Lord Jesus Christ, for You have vouchsafed to remember me, Your poorest servant, and sometimes You comfort me with Your gracious presence, who am unworthy of all comfort. I bless You and glorify You always, with Your only-begotten Son and the Holy Spirit, without end.

O my Lord God, most faithful Lover, when You come into my heart, all within me rejoices. You are my glory and the joy of my heart, my hope and my whole refuge in all my troubles. Because I am yet feeble in love and imperfect in virtue, I therefore have need to have more comfort and more help from You. Vouchsafe, therefore, frequently to visit me, and to instruct me with Your holy teachings. Deliver me from all evil passions, and heal my sick heart from all earthly inclinations, so that I may be inwardly healed and purged from all inordinate affections and vices, and be made ready and able to love You, strong to suffer for You, and firm to persevere in You.

Love is a great and good thing, and alone makes heavy burdens light and bears in equal balance things pleasing and displeasing. Love bears a heavy burden and does not feel it, and love makes bitter things tasteful and sweet. The noble love of Jesus perfectly imprinted in man's soul makes a man do great things, and stirs him always to desire perfection and to grow more and more in grace and goodness.

Love will always have a man's mind raised to God and not occupied with the things of the world. Love will also be free from all worldly affection, so that the inward sight of the soul is not darkened or hindered, and a man's affection toward heavenly things is not banished from his free will by an inordinate winning or losing of worldly things. Nothing, therefore, is sweeter than love; nothing higher, nothing stronger, nothing larger, nothing more joyful, nothing fuller, nothing better, in heaven or on earth, for love descends from God, and may not finally rest in anything lower than God. Such a lover flies high; he runs swiftly, he is merry in God, he is free in soul. He gives all for all, and has all in all, for he rests in one high Goodness above all things, from whom all goodness flows and proceeds. He beholds not only the gifts, but the Giver above all gifts.

Love knows no measure, but is fervent without measure. It feels no burden; it regards no labor; it desires more than it can obtain. It complains of no impossibility, for it thinks all things that can be done for its Beloved are possible and lawful. So, love does many great things and brings them to completion—things in which he who is no lover faints and fails.

Love wakes much and sleeps little and, in sleeping, does not sleep. It faints and is not weary; it is restricted in its liberty and is in great freedom. It sees reasons to fear and does not fear, but, like an ember or a spark of fire, flames always upward, by the fervor of its love, toward God, and through the special help of grace is delivered from all perils and dangers.

He who is thus a spiritual lover knows well what that voice means which says: You, Lord God, are my whole love and my desire. You are all mine, and I all Yours. Dissolve my heart into Your love so that I may know how sweet it is to serve You and how joyful it is to praise You, and to be as though I were all melded into Your love. Oh, I am urged on by love and go far above myself because of the great fervor I feel through Your unspeakable goodness. I shall sing to You the song of love; I shall follow You, my Beloved, in flights of thought wherever You go, and my soul will never be weary in praising You with the joyful songs of spiritual love that I will sing to you. I will love You more than myself, and will not love myself except for you; and I shall love all others in You and for You, as the law of love which You give commands. Love is swift, pure, humble, joyful and glad, strong, patient, faithful, wise, forbearing, manly, and never seeks itself or its own will. Whenever a man seeks himself he falls from love. Love is circumspect, meek, righteous; not weak, not flighty or concerned with vain things. It is sober, chaste, firm, quiet, and well poised in its outward display. Love is subject and obedient to authority, low and despicable in its own sight, devout and thankful to God. Love always trusts and hopes in God, even when it has but little devotion and little savor of God. Without some sorrow and pain, no man can live in love.

He who is not always ready to suffer and to stand completely at the will of his beloved is not worthy to be called a lover, for it behooves a lover gladly to suffer all hard and bitter things for his beloved, and not to fall from love because of any irksome thing that may befall him.

6. Of the Proof of a True Lover of God

My son, says our Saviour Christ, you are not yet a strong and a wise lover.

Why, Lord?

Because of a little adversity you soon leave off what you had begun in My service, and with great yearning you seek outward consolation. But a strong and faithful lover of God stands unshaken in all adversities, and gives little heed to the deceitful persuasions of the enemy. As I please such a lover in prosperity, so I do not displease him in adversity. A wise lover does not so much consider the gift of his lover as he does the love of the giver. He regards more the love than the gift, and accounts all gifts little in comparison with his beloved, who gives them to him. A noble lover does not rest in the gift, but rests in Me, above all gifts.

But all is not lost, though you sometimes feel less devotion to Me and to my saints than you would feel. On the other hand, the sweet spiritual desire you sometimes feel toward your Lord Jesus is the manifest gift of grace given for your comfort in this life, and a taste of heavenly glory in the life to come. But it is not good for you to lean overmuch on such comforts, for they easily come and go, according to the will of the Giver. To strive always without ceasing against all evil motions of sin and to despise all suggestions of the enemy is a token of perfect love, of great merit and singular grace.

Let no vanities or strange fantasies trouble you, no

matter what they concern. Keep your intention and your purpose always whole and strong toward Me, and do not think that it is an illusion you are suddenly lifted up to sublime thoughts, and you are soon after turned again to your first levity of heart; for you suffer such levity of heart against your will rather than with your will, and so, if you are displeased by it, it will be of great merit for you, and no loss.

I know, says our Lord, that the old ancient enemy, the devil, will try to hinder your good will and to extinguish the good desire you have toward Me and to all goodness, as far as he can. And he will also hinder you from all good works and devout exercises, if he can, that is to say, from the honor and worship you are bound to give Me and My saints. He will try to hinder you from the remembrance of My Passion, and from the recollection of your own sins, from a diligent keeping of your heart in good meditation, and from a steadfast purpose to advance in virtue. He will also put into your mind many idle thoughts, to make you soon weary with prayer and with reading, and with all other good, virtuous works. A humble confession displeases him much; if he can, he will hinder a man from making his confession. Do not believe him, and do not regard him, though he assail you ever so much. Make all the devil's malice turn back upon him and say to him: Go from me, you wicked spirit, and be ashamed, for you are foul and ugly who would bring such things into my mind. Go from me, you false deceiver of mankind. You shall never have part in me, for my Saviour Jesus stands beside me like a mighty warrior and a strong companion, and you shall fly away to your confusion. I had rather suffer the most cruel death than consent to your malicious stories. Be still, you cursed fiend, and cease your malice, for I will never assent to you, though you vex me ever so much. Our Lord is my light and my salvation, whom shall I dread? He is the defender of my life; what shall

I fear? If a host of men arise against me, my heart will not dread, for God is my Helper and my Redeemer.

Then, says our Lord again to such a soul: Strive always like a true knight against all the stirrings of the enemy, and if sometimes through your frailty you are overcome, rise soon again, and take more strength than you had first, and trust truly to have more grace and more comfort from God than you had before. But beware always of vainglory and pride, for by them many persons have fallen into great errors and into great blindness of soul to such an extent that their ill has been well nigh incurable. Let the fall and ruin of such proud folk therefore be a great example and a matter of perpetual humility to you—such proud folk who have foolishly presumed of themselves, and have in the end perished by their presumption.

7. How Grace Is to be Kept Close through the Virtue of Humility

My son, it is much more expedient and the surer way for you that you hide the grace of devotion and speak not much of it, nor much regard it; but belittle yourself the more because of it, and think yourself unworthy of any such gracious gift from God. And it is not good to cling much to such affections as may soon be turned into the contrary. When you have the grace of devotion, consider how wretched and how needy you were wont to be when you had no such grace. The profit and increase of spiritual life comes not only when you have devotion, but rather, when you can humbly and patiently bear the withdrawal and the absence of devotion, yet not cease your prayers or leave undone your other customary good works. As far as lies in you, do your best in your accustomed prayers and good deeds, and do not forget your duties, or be negligent because of any dullness or disquiet of mind.

Nevertheless, there are many persons who, when any adversity befalls them, soon grow impatient and become very dull and slow to do any good deed, and so hinder themselves greatly. The way he will take does not lie in the power of man; it is in the grace of God alone to dispose all this according to His will, and to send comfort when He will, and as much as He will, and to whom He will, as it shall please Him, and not otherwise. Some reckless people, through an indiscreet desire to obtain the grace of devotion, have destroyed themselves, for they desired to do more than they had power to do. They would not acknowledge the measure of their gifts, or the littleness of their own strength, but chose to follow the pride of their heart rather than the judgment of reason. And because they presumed to do greater things than were pleasing to God, they soon lost the grace they had before. They were left needy and without comfort, who thought to have built their nest in heaven. And so they were taught not to presume of themselves, but humbly to trust in God and in His goodness.

Those, too, who are beginners and still lack experience in spiritual toil may easily err and be deceived unless they are ruled by the counsel of others. And if they feel the need to follow their own counsel and in no ways be shaken from it, it will be very dangerous to them in the end. It is not often seen that those who are wise and learned in their own sight will be humbly ruled or governed by others. Therefore, it is better to have little learning with humility than great learning and great pleasure in it; it is better to have a little learning with grace than much learning of which you are proud.

He does not act discreetly who in time of devotion gives himself to all spiritual happiness and, as it were, to a heavenly gladness, forgetting his former desolation and the humble fear of God. Neither does he act well or virtuously who, in time of trouble or in any manner of adversity, acts with too little hope, and does not think of Me with all the trust he ought. He who in time of peace and of spiritual comfort thinks himself supremely secure will, in time of battle and of temptation, commonly be found all too dejected and fearful. If you could always remain humble and little in your own sight, and could govern well the motions of your own soul, you would not so swiftly fall into presumption or despair, or so easily offend Almighty God. And so, this is good and wholesome counsel: When you have the spirit of fervor, think how you will act when the fervor is past; when it is past, think that the fervor, which to My honor and for your testing I have withdrawn for a time, may soon come to you again. And it is more profitable to you to be so tested than always to have things prosper according to your will.

Merit is not to be thought great in any person because he has many visions or many spiritual comforts, or because he has clear understanding of Scripture, or is set in a high position. But if he is firmly grounded in humility and is filled with charity; if he seeks wholly the worship of God and regards himself in nothing; if he can in his heart fully despise himself and desire as well to be despised by others, then he may have good trust that he has gained somewhat in grace, and that he will in the end have the great reward of God for his good toil.

8. How through Humility We Should Think Ourselves Mean and Abject in the Sight of God

Shall I, Lord Jesus, dare speak to You, I who am but dust and ashes? Truly, if I think myself any better than ashes and dust, You stand against me, and my own sins also bear witness against me. That I cannot deny. But if I despise myself and set myself at naught and think myself but ashes and dust, as I am, then Your grace will be close to me and the light of true understanding will enter into my heart, so that all presumption and pride in me will be drowned in the valley of meekness, through perfect knowledge of my wretchedness.

Through humility You will show me what I am, what I have been, and from whence I came, for I am nothing, and did not know. If I am left to myself, then I am nothing, and all is frailty and imperfection; but if You vouchsafe a little to regard me, soon I am made strong and am filled with a new joy. It is a marvel that I, a wretch, am so soon lifted up from my instability into the contemplation of heavenly things, and that I am so lovingly supported by You, who of myself always fall before worldly attractions. But Your love, Lord, causes all this, Your love which goes before me, and helps me in all my necessities, and keeps me carefully from all perils and dangers into which I am daily likely to fall. I have lost You, and myself as well, by the inordinate love I have had for myself; in seeking You again, I have found both You and myself. Therefore, I will from now on more deeply set myself at naught and more diligently seek You than I have done in times past. You, Lord Jesus, You deal with me above all my merits, and above all that I can possibly ask or desire.

May You be blessed in all Your works, O Lord, for, though I am unworthy of any good thing, Your goodness never ceases to do well by me, and to many others who are unfriendly to You and who are even turned fully against You. Turn us, therefore, O Lord, turn us to Yourself again, that we may be henceforth loving, thankful, humble, and devout to You, for You are our help, You are our strength and all our virtue in body and in soul; and no other except You. To You, therefore, be joy and glory everlasting in the bliss of heaven.

9. How All Things Are to be Referred to God as to the End of Every Work

My son, says our Saviour Christ, I must be the end of all your works, if you desire to be happy and blessed. If you refer all goodness to Me, from whom all goodness comes, then all your inward affections will be purified and made clean, which otherwise would be evil and centered on yourself and other creatures. If you seek yourself as the goal of your work in anything, you soon fall short in your activities, and become dry and barren of all the refreshment of grace. And so, you must refer all things to Me, for I give all. Behold all things as they are, flowing and springing forth from My sovereign goodness, and reduce all things to Me as to their original beginning. From Me both great and small, poor and rich, draw the water of life as from a quick-springing well.

He who serves Me freely and with good will receives grace for grace. However, he who glorifies himself, or who will fully rejoice in anything except Me, will not be established in perfect joy or enlarged in soul, but will be hindered and straitened in many ways from true freedom of spirit. You therefore should ascribe no goodness to yourself, or think that any person has any goodness of himself. But you should always yield the goodness to Me, without whom man has nothing. I have given all, and I will have all back again, and with great strictness will I look for your thanks for what I have given.

This is the truth by which all kinds of vainglory and pride of heart are driven away. If heavenly grace and perfect charity enter into your heart, then no envy or disquiet of mind or any private love will rule in you, for the charity of God will overcome all, and will expand and enkindle all the powers of your soul. And so, if you understand properly, you will never rejoice save in Me, and in Me alone will you trust, for no man is good, but God alone, who is above all things to be honored and above all things to be blessed.

10. *That It Is Sweet and Pleasant to Serve God, and to Forsake the World*

Now I shall speak yet again to You, my Lord Jesus, and not cease. And I shall say to the ears of my Lord: My God and King who is in heaven, oh, how great is the abundance of Your sweetness which you have hidden and reserved for those who fear you! But what is it, then, to those who love You and serve You with all their hearts? Truly, it is the unspeakable sweetness of contemplation, which You give those who love You. In this, Lord, You have made most manifest the sweetness of Your charity to me, namely, that when I was not, you made me; when I wandered far from You, You brought me again to serve You and commanded me to love You.

O Fountain of everlasting love, what shall I say of You? How can I forget You, who have vouchsafed to remember me so lovingly? When I was on the verge of perishing, You showed Your mercy to me above all I could have thought or desired, and You sent me Your grace and Your love, above all my merits. But what shall I give You in return for all this goodness? It is not given to all men to forsake the world and to take on a solitary life, solely to serve You. Yet it is no great burden to serve You, whom every creature is bound to serve. It ought not, therefore, seem any great thing to me to serve You; rather, it should seem a great wonder to me that You will deign to receive so poor and so unworthy a creature as I am into Your service, and that You will join me to Your well-beloved servants.

Lo, Lord, all that I have and all with which I serve

You are Yours, yet Your goodness is such that You serve me rather than I You. Behold, heaven and earth, planets and stars and all that is in them, which You have created to serve man, are ready at Your bidding and do daily what You have commanded. And You have also ordained that the angels minister to man. Above all this, You have deigned to serve man Yourself, and have promised to give Yourself to him.

What, then, shall I return You for this thousandfold goodness? Would to God that I might serve You all the days of my life—at least that I might one day be able to render You faithful service—for You are worthy of all honor, service, and praise forever. You are my Lord and my God, and I am your poor servant, bound most before all others to love and praise You, and I ought never to grow weary in praising. This is what I ask and what I desire: that I may always glorify You and praise You. Vouchsafe, therefore, most merciful Lord, to supply whatever is wanting in me, for it is great honor to serve You, and for Your love to despise all earthly things. They will have great grace who freely submit themselves to Your holy service, and they will find, too, the most sweet consolation of the Holy Spirit, and will have great freedom of spirit who here forsake all worldly business and choose a hard and a strict life in this world for Your Name.

O glad and joyful service of God, by which a man is made free and holy and blessed in the sight of God; O holy state of religion, which makes a man like to the angels, pleasing to God, feared by the wicked spirits and most highly praised by all faithful people. O service much to be embraced and always to be desired, by which high goodness is won and everlasting joy and gladness without end is gained.

11. *That the Desires of the Heart Ought to be Well Examined and Well Moderated*

My son, says our Lord, it behooves you to learn many things which you have not yet learned well.

What are they, Lord?

That you order your desires and your affections wholly after My pleasure, and that you be not a lover of yourself, but an eager follower of My will in all things. I know well that desires often move you to this thing or to that, but consider well whether you are moved chiefly for My honor or for your own. If I am the cause and goal, you will be well content, whatever I do with you. But if anything of your own will remains in your heart, it is that which hinders you.

Take care, therefore, not to lean too much toward your own desire without My counsel, lest, perhaps, what first pleased you bring you regret and displeasure in the end. Every affection and desire of man's heart that seems good and holy is not at once to be followed, nor is every unattractive affection or desire quickly to be refused. It is sometimes very expedient for a man to restrain his affections and desires, though they are good, lest, perhaps, by his importunity he fall into disquiet of mind, or be a hindrance to others or be hindered by others, and so fail in his actions. Sometimes it behooves us to use, as it were, violence to ourselves, and strongly to resist and break down our sensual appetite, and not to regard what the flesh would or would not, but always to take heed that the flesh be made subject to the will of the spirit, and that it be chastised and compelled to serve, until it is ready for all things that the soul commands, and until it can learn to be content with a little and to delight in simple things, not murmuring or objecting because of any contrary thing that may befall it.

12. That We Should Keep Patience, and Continually Strive against All Concupiscence

O Lord my God, patience is very necessary for me, for many disturbing things occur daily in this life. I see well that however I govern myself so as to have peace, my life cannot be without some struggle and sorrow.

My son, what you say is true. And therefore I do not will you to have peace that is free from temptations, or does not feel some contradiction. But I will that you think and believe that you have found peace, when you have many troubles and are tried by many unpleasant things in this world. If you say that you cannot bear such things, how, then, will you suffer the fires of purgatory? Of two evils, the lesser is to be chosen; suffer patiently, therefore, the small pains of this world, so that you may hereafter escape the greater pains in the world to come.

Do you think that worldly men suffer little or nothing? You certainly will find no one without some trouble, though you seek out the most privileged of people. But perhaps you shall say to Me that they have so many delights and follow their own pleasures so much that they weigh all their adversities but little. I know well it is as you say, that they have all they can desire. But how long will it endure, do you think? Truly, it will suddenly vanish away, like smoke in the air, so that no remembrance of past joys will be left. Even when they lived, they were not without great bitterness and grief, for the very things in which they had greatest pleasure often gave them great trouble and pain afterwards. And it was most just that, inasmuch as they sought delight and pleasure inordinately, they should not get their full desire in such pleasure save with great bitterness and sorrow. Oh, how short, how false, and how ill-ordered are all the pleasures of this world! Surely, worldly people do not perceive this because of excesses and blindness of heart, and they will not perceive it, for to gain a little pleasure in this corruptible life they run headlong, like dumb beasts, to everlasting death.

Therefore, my son, do not follow your concupiscence, but turn quickly away from your own will. Delight in God and fix your will strongly in Him, and He will give you the desires of your heart. If you will have consolation abundantly, and will receive the sure and faithful comfort that comes from God, dispose yourself fully to despise this world, and put aside completely all inordinate pleasures, and you will plentifully share the comfort of God. The more you withdraw yourself from the consolation of all creatures, the sweeter and more blessed consolations you will receive from your Creator.

But truly, you cannot at first arrive at such consolations without struggle and labor that must precede. Your old habits will somewhat forestall you, but better habits can overcome the old ones. The flesh will murmur against you, but it can be restrained by fervor of spirit. The old ancient enemy, the devil, will hinder you if he can, but by devout prayer he will be driven away, and by good bodily and spiritual labor his way will be blocked, and he will not dare come near you.

13. Of the Obedience of a Humble Subject, after the Example of Our Lord Jesus Christ

My son, says our Saviour Christ, he who labors to withdraw himself from obedience withdraws himself from grace; he who seeks to have private possessions loses the things that are in common.

If a man cannot gladly submit himself to his superiors, it is a sign that his flesh is not yet fully obedient to the spirit, but that it often rebels and murmurs. Therefore, if you desire to overcome yourself, and to make your flesh humbly obey the will of the spirit, learn first gladly to obey your superiors. The outward enemy is the sooner overcome if the inner man, that is, the soul, is not enfeebled or weakened. There is no worse and no more threatening enemy to your soul than yourself, if your flesh is not submissive to the will of the spirit. It behooves you, therefore, to have a true deprecation and contempt of yourself, if you would prevail against your flesh and blood. But, insomuch as you yet love yourself inordinately, you fear to resign your will wholly to another man's will.

But what great thing is it to you, who are but dust and nothing, if you submit yourself to man for My sake, when I, who am Almighty and the Most High God, Creator of all things, submitted Myself humbly to man for your sake? I made Myself the humblest and lowest of all men, so that you would learn to overcome your pride through My humility. Learn, therefore, you who are but ashes, to be docile; learn, you who are dust and earth, to be humble for my sake; learn to break your own will and to be subject to all from the heart. Rise in great wrath against yourself, and do not suffer pride to reign in you, but show yourself to be in your own sight little and obedient. O vain man, what have you to complain of? O foul sinner, what can you justly say against those who rebuke you, since you have so often offended God and have so often deserved the pains of hell? Nevertheless, because your soul is precious in My sight, My merciful eye has spared you, so that you should thereby know the great love I have for you, and be the more thankful to Me in return, and give yourself to perfect and true humility. Be ready in your heart patiently to suffer contempt and derision for My sake, whenever they happen to fall to your lot.

14. Of the Secret and Hidden Judgments of God to be Considered So That We Do Not Become Proud of Our Good Deeds

Lord, You sound forth Your judgments terribly upon me, and fill my body and my bones with great fear and dread. My soul trembles sorely, for I am greatly bewildered when I see that even the heavens are not clean in Your sight. Since You found sin in the angels and did not spare them, what shall become of me, who am but a mean person? Stars fell from heaven; what should I presume who am but dust and ashes? Sometimes, people who seem to have great works of virtue have fallen low indeed and I have seen those who were fed with the bread of angels afterwards delight in the food of swine, that is, in fleshly pleasure.

Wherefore, it may be well said and found true that there is no holiness or goodness in us if You withdraw Your merciful hand. No wisdom can benefit us if You, Lord, do not govern it, nor can any strength help if You cease to preserve us; no chastity can be secure if You, Lord, do not defend it; no sure protection can profit us if You, Lord, do not keep watch upon us; for, if we are forsaken by You, we are soon lost and perish. But if You visit us a little with Your grace, we quickly live and are lifted up again. We are unstable, but by You we are made firm; we are cold and dull, but by You we are stirred to fervor of spirit.

Oh, how humbly and how abjectly ought I therefore estimate myself. How much ought I, in my heart, despise myself, even though I am considered ever so holy and good in the sight of the world, and how deeply ought I submit myself to Your deep and profound judgments, since I find in myself nothing but naught and naught. O substance that cannot be weighed! O sea that cannot be sailed! In You and by You I find that my substance is nothing, and above all, nothing.

Where, now, is the shadow of this worldly glory, and where is the trust that I had in it? Truly, it is vanished away, through the depths of Your secret and hidden judgment upon me. What is flesh in Your sight? How may the clay glorify itself against its Maker? How may he be deceived by vain praises whose heart in truth is subject to God? All the world may not lift him up into pride whom Truth, that is, God, has made perfectly subject to Himself; nor may he be deceived by any flattery who puts all his whole trust in God. He sees well that they who speak are vain and naught, and that they shall shortly fail with the sound of their words, but that the truth of God abides always.

15. *How a Man Should Order Himself in His Desires*

My son, says our Saviour Christ, you should speak thus in everything that you desire: Lord, if it be Your will, be it done as I ask, and if it be to Your praise, let it be fulfilled in Your Name. And if you see that it is good and profitable to me, give me grace to use it to Your honor; if You know it to be hurtful to me, and not profitable to the health of my soul, then take away from me such desire.

Not every desire comes from the Holy Spirit, though it seem right and just. It is sometimes quite hard to judge whether a good or an evil spirit moves you to this or to that, or whether you are moved by your own spirit. Many are deceived in the end, who first appeared to have been moved by the Holy Spirit.

Therefore, with fear of God and with humility of heart, you should desire and ask whatever comes into your mind to be desired and asked. And with a complete forsaking of yourself, commit all things to God and say: Lord, You know what is most profitable to me; do this or that according to Your will. Give me what You will, as much as You will, and when You will. Do with me as You know what is best to be done, as it shall please You, and as it shall be most to Your honor. Put me where You will, and freely do with me in all things according to Your will. I am Your creature, and in Your hands; lead me and turn me where You will. Lo, I am Your servant, ready to do all things that You command, for I do not desire to live to myself, but to You. Would to God that I might live worthily and profitably, and to Your honor.

A Prayer that the Will of God Always Be Fulfilled

Most benign Lord Jesus, grant me Your grace, that it may always be with me and work with me and preserve me unto the end. Grant that I may always desire and will what is most pleasing and acceptable to You. Let Your will be my will, and let my will always follow Your will and best conform with it. Let there be always in me one will and one desire with You, and grant that I may have no power to will or not to will except as You will or do not will. Grant that I may die to all things in the world, and that for You I may love to be despised and be a man unknown in this world. Grant me, also, above all things that can be desired, that I may rest in You and fully in You bring peace to my heart. You, Lord, are the truest peace of the heart, and the perfect rest of body and soul, and without You all things weary and disturb. Wherefore, in that peace which is in You, one high, one blessed and one endless Goodness, shall I always find my rest. So be it.

16. That the Truest Solace and Comfort Is in God

Whatever I can desire or think for my comfort I do not expect here, but I trust to have it hereafter. If I alone might have all the solace and comfort of this world, and might use the delights of this world according to my own desire and without sin, it is certain that they would not long endure. And so, my soul cannot be fully comforted or perfectly refreshed, except in God alone, who is the Comforter of the poor in spirit and the Embracer of the humble and low in heart. Await, my soul, await the promise of God, and you will have abundance of all goodness in heaven. If you inordinately covet these present goods, you will lose eternal goods. So, use present goods properly, but yearn for eternal goods.

You can in no manner be satisfied with temporal goods, for you were not created to find your rest in them. If you alone might have all the goods that were ever created, you would not therefore be happy and blessed. Your blessedness and your full happiness stand only in God, who has made all things from nothing. The felicity that is praised by the foolish lovers of the world is not true felicity, but only such as good Christian men and women hope to have in the joy of heaven, and as some spiritual persons, clean and pure in heart, sometimes taste here in this present life—those whose conversation is in heaven. All worldly solace, and all man's comfort, is vain and short, but that comfort is blessed and certain which is perceived by truth inwardly in the heart.

A devout follower of God bears about with him his Comforter, that is, Jesus, and says to Him: My Lord Jesus, I beseech You to be with me in every place and at every time, that I may have the special grace for Your love gladly to lack all man's solace. And if Your solace be wanting to me also, grant that Your will and Your just testing and assaying of me may be to me a singular comfort and a high solace. You will not always be angry with me, nor will You threaten me forever. So may it be.

17. *That All Our Study and Busyness of Mind Ought to be Put in God*

My Son, says our Lord to His servant, suffer Me to do with you what I will, for I know what is best and most expedient for you. You work in many things according to your human reason, and so your affection and your worldly disposition move you, and so you easily err and are deceived.

O Lord, all You say is true. Your providence is much better for me than all I can say or do for myself. And so it can well be said and found true that he stands very uncertainly who does not set all his trust in You. Therefore, Lord, while my intention abides steadfast and firm, do with me in all things as it pleases You, for all that You do cannot be otherwise than good. If it is Your will that I be in light, be You blessed. If it is Your will that I be in darkness, be You also blessed. If You deign to comfort me, be You highly blessed; if You will me to live in trouble and without all comfort, be You in like manner much blessed.

My son, so it ought to be with you. If you will walk with Me you must be as ready to suffer as to rejoice, and as gladly to be needy and poor as to be wealthy and rich.

Lord, I will gladly suffer for You whatever You will to come upon me. With equal thanks will I take from Your hand good and bad, bitter and sweet, gladness and sorrow. And I will thank You from the heart for all that shall befall me. Keep me from sin, Lord, and I will fear neither death nor hell. Do not blot my name from the book of life, and whatever trouble befalls me will not grieve me.

18. *That All Temporal Miseries Are Gladly to be Borne through the Example of Christ*

My son, says our Lord, I descended from heaven and for your help I have taken your miseries, not compelled to do so by necessity, but by My charity, so that you should learn with Me to have patience and not to refuse to bear the miseries and the wretchedness of this life, as I have done for you. From the first hour of My birth unto My death upon the cross, I was never without some sorrow or pain. I had great lack of temporal things; I heard great complaints made against me; I suffered humbly many shames and rebukes. For My benefits I received unkindness; for My miracles, blasphemies; for My true doctrine, many reproofs.

O Lord, since You were found patient in Your life, fulfilling in Your patience most especially the will of Your Father, it is fitting that I, a most wretched sinner, should bear myself patiently according to Your will in all things, and that I should, for my own salvation, bear the burden of this corruptible life as long as You will it. Though this life is irksome and a heavy burden to the soul, it is now through Your grace made very meritorious. And by Your example and the example of Your holy saints, this life is now made for weak people more bearable and more clear, and much more full of consolation than it was under the Old Law, when so few desired to seek it because the gates of heaven were shut and the way to heaven dark. And even those who were then righteous and were destined to be saved could never have come there before Your blessed Passion and Death.

Oh, what thanks for this am I not bound to give You, who so lovingly have deigned to show me and all faithful persons who will follow You the very true and direct way to Your kingdom. Your holy light is our way, and by Your patience we will walk to You who are our Head and our Governor. And had You not, Lord, gone before and showed us the way, who would have bent himself to follow You? Oh, how many would have lagged behind, if they had not seen Your blessed example going before. We are yet slow and dull, though we have seen and heard Your miracles and doctrine. What, then, would we have been if we had seen no such light going before us? Surely, we would have fixed our minds and our love fully on worldly things, but now, from them, Lord, may Your great goodness preserve us.

19.   Of Patient Suffering of Injuries and Wrongs and Who Is Truly Patient

My son, what is it you say? Why do you thus complain? Cease, cease, complain no more. Consider My Passion and the passion of My saints, and you will see well that what you suffer for Me is very little. You have not yet suffered to the shedding of your blood, and surely you have suffered little in comparison with those who have suffered so many great things from Me in time past, and those who have been so strongly tempted, so grievously troubled and in so many ways put to the test. It behooves you, therefore, to remember the great, serious things others have suffered for Me, so that you may the more lightly bear your little grief. And if they do not seem little to you, take care that your impatience is not the cause. Nevertheless, whether they are little or great, study always to bear them patiently, if you can, without begrudging or complaining. The better you dispose yourself to suffer them, the more wisely you act, and the more merit will you have, and because of your good disposition and your good will, your burden will be lighter.

You will never say: I cannot suffer this thing from such a person, nor is it expected of me to suffer it. He has done me great wrong, and accused me of things I never thought; but from another man I am willing to suffer for what I thought. Such kind of utterance is not good, for it does not consider the virtue of patience, or by whom patience shall be crowned; rather, it considers the persons and the offenses done.

And so, he is not truly patient who will suffer only as much as he pleases, or from whom he pleases. A truly patient man gives no heed from whom he suffers, whether from his superior or from his equal or from someone below him, or whether he is a good and a holy man, or an evil and an unworthy man. But whenever any adversity or wrong befalls him, whatever it be, no matter from whom it comes or how often it comes, he takes all faithfully from the hand of God, and accounts it as a rich gift and a great benefit, for he knows that there is nothing a man can suffer for God that goes without great merit.

Be ready for battle, therefore, if you would have victory. Without battle you cannot come to the crown of patience, and if you will not suffer, you refuse to be crowned. Wherefore, if you desire to be crowned, resist strongly and suffer patiently, for without labor no man can come to rest, and without battle no man can come to victory.

O Lord Jesus, make possible to me by grace what is impossible to me by nature. You know well that I can suffer little, and that I am soon cast down by a little adversity. Wherefore, I beseech You that hereafter I may love and desire trouble and adversity for Your Name; truly, to suffer and to be troubled for You is very good and profitable for the health of my soul.

20. *Of the Acknowledgment of Our Own Infirmities and the Miseries of This Life*

I shall acknowledge against myself all my unrighteousness, and I shall confess to You, Lord, all the instability of my heart. Often it is but a little thing that casts me down and makes me dull and slow to all good works. Sometimes I resolve to stand strongly, but, when a little temptation comes, it is a great anguish and grief to me. Sometimes from a very little thing a grievous temptation rises. And when I think that I am somewhat secure and that, as it seems, I have the upper hand, suddenly I feel myself all but overcome by a light temptation.

Behold, therefore, good Lord, behold my weakness and my frailty, best known to You above all others. Have mercy on me, Lord, and deliver me from the foul dregs of sin, so that my feet may never be fixed in them. But it often troubles me sorely, and in a way confounds me before You, that I am so unstable and so weak, so frail in resisting my passions. And though they do not always draw me to give consent, their cruel assaults are very grievous to me, so that it is wearisome to me to live in such a struggle. Yet, such a struggle is not all unprofitable to me, because by it I know my own infirmities better, for I see that such wicked imaginings rise in me much sooner than they depart. But would to God that You, most strong God of Israel, lover of all faithful souls, would deign to behold my sorrow and labor, and that you would assist me, Your poorest servant, in all that I have to do. Strengthen me, Lord, with heavenly strength, so that neither the old enemy, the devil, against whom I must fight endlessly while I live in this miserable life, nor my wretched flesh, not yet fully subject to the spirit, have power or domination over me.

But alas, what kind of life is this, where trouble and misery are not wanting, where every place is full of snares and mortal enemies? For one trouble or temptation that departs, another comes, and while the first conflict yet endures, many others suddenly rise, more than can be imagined. How, therefore, can this life be loved which experiences such bitterness and is subject to so many miseries? And how may it be called a life when it brings forth so many deaths and so many spiritual plagues? Yet it is delighted in by many persons. The world is often charged with being deceitful and vain, yet it is not easily forsaken, especially when the concupiscences of the flesh are allowed to rule. Some things stir a man to love the world, and some to despise it. The concupiscence of the flesh, the concupiscence of the eye, and the pride of the heart stir a man to love the world, but the pains and miseries that follow cause hatred of it and weariness with it.

But alas, for sorrow, a little pleasure overcomes the minds of those who are too much given to love the world, and drives out of their hearts all heavenly desires, to such an extent that many account it as a very joy of paradise to live under such sensual pleasures; that is because they have neither seen nor tasted the sweetness in God nor the inward gladness that comes from virtue. But they who perfectly despise the world and study to live under holy discipline are not ignorant of the heavenly sweetness promised to spiritual men, and they see also how deeply the world errs, and how grievously in so many ways it is deceived.

21. *How a Man Should Rest in God above All Things*

Above all things and in all things rest, my soul, in my Lord God, for He is the eternal rest of all angels and saints.

Give me, Lord Jesus, special grace to rest in You above all creatures, above all health and beauty, above all glory and honor, above all dignity and power, above all wisdom and prudence, above all riches and skills, above all gladness of body and soul, above all fame and praise, above all sweetness and consolation, above all hope and promise, above all merit and desire, above all gifts and rewards that You may give or send, except Yourself, and above all joy and mirth that man's heart or man can conceive or feel, and above all angels or archangels and all the company of heavenly spirits as well, above all things visible and invisible, above all things that are not Yourself.

You, Lord God, are most good, most high, most mighty, most sufficient and most full of goodness, most sweet, most consoling, most fair, most loving, most noble, and most glorious above all things. In You all goodness is together, perfectly and fully—has been and will be. Therefore, whatever You give me, beside Yourself, is little and insufficient to me, for my heart cannot rest, or be fully brought to peace, so that it may ascend above all gifts and above all manner of created things, save in You.

O my Lord Jesus Christ, most loving Spouse, most pure Lover and Governor of every creature, who will give me wings of perfect liberty, so that I may fly high and rest in You. Oh, when shall I fully tend to You and see and feel how sweet You are? When shall I recollect myself so perfectly that I shall not, for Your love, recognize myself, but You alone above myself and above all physical things? You will visit me in such manner as You visit Your faithful lovers. Now, I often mourn and complain of the miseries of this life, and with sorrow and woe bear them with truly great melancholy, for many evil things happen daily in this life which trouble me and greatly darken my understanding. They hinder me greatly, and put my mind away from You, and encumber me so in many ways that I cannot have a free mind and clear desire toward You, or have the sweet embrace that is always present to Your blessed saints. Wherefore, I beseech You, Lord, that the sighing and the inward desire of my heart, together with my many desolations, may somewhat move You and incline You to hear me.

O Jesus, the light and brightness of everlasting glory, the joy and comfort of all Christian people who walk and labor like pilgrims in the wickedness of this world, my heart cries to You by silent desires, without voice; my silence speaks to You and says: How long does my Lord God delay to come? Truly, I trust that He will shortly come to me, His poorest servant, and comfort me and make me joyful and glad in Himself, and deliver me from all anguish and sorrow. Come, Lord, come, for without You I have no glad day or hour. You are all my joy and gladness, and without You my soul is barren and empty. I am a wretch and, as it were, in prison and bound with fetters until You, through the light of Your gracious presence, deign to visit me and to refresh me, to bring me again to liberty of spirit and to show me Your favorable and lovely countenance. Let others seek what they will, but truly, there is nothing I shall seek, or that will please me but You, my Lord God, my hope and everlasting help. I shall not cease my prayer until Your grace return to me, and until You speak inwardly to my soul and say: Lo, I am here; I am come to you because you have called Me. Your tears and the desires of your heart, your humility and your contrition, have bowed Me down and brought Me to you.

And I shall say in return: Lord, I have called You and I have desired to have You. I am ready to forsake all things for You, for You first stirred me to seek You. Wherefore, be You always blessed, who have shown such goodness to me according to the multitude of Your mercies. What has Your servant, Lord, to do or say more, save to humble himself before Your majesty and ever to have in mind his own iniquities? There is none like to You, Lord, in heaven or on earth. Your works are good, Your judgments are wise and just, and Your providence governs all things. Wherefore, to You, who are the wisdom of the Father, be everlasting joy and glory. I humbly beseech You that my body and my soul, my heart and my tongue and all your creatures may always praise You and bless You.

22. *Of Remembering the Great and Manifold Blessings of God*

Open my heart, Lord, to behold Your laws, and teach me to walk in Your commandments. Give me grace to know and understand Your will, and with great reverence and loving consideration to remember Your many benefits, so that from henceforth I may return You due thanks for them. But I know and confess it as truth that I am not yet able to give fitting thanks for the least benefit You have given me, for I am less than the least gift You have bestowed. When I behold Your nobility and Your worthiness, my spirit fears and trembles sorely before their greatness.

O Lord, all that we have in body and in soul, within or without, naturally or supernaturally, are Your benefits, and openly show You from whom we have received such gifts to be a blessed and a good benefactor. And though one has received more, and another less, they are all Your gifts; without You the least cannot be possessed. He who has received more may not rightly glorify himself more because of that, as though he had gained it by his own merits, nor exalt himself above others, nor disdain others, nor despise his inferiors because of it. He is greatest and most acceptable to You who ascribes least to himself, and who, because of such gifts, is more humble and more devout in returning thanks to You for them. He who through humility can estimate himself most unworthy of all is the more worthy to receive from Your hand the greater gift. And he who has received fewer gifts ought not therefore to be sad, or envious of those who have received greater, but he ought therefore to lift his mind upward to You, and highly to praise Your Name, because You so liberally, so lovingly, and so freely, without respect to persons, divide Your gifts among Your people. All things come from You, and therefore You are in all things to be blessed. You know what is expedient to be given to every person, and why one has less and another more. It is not for us to reason or to judge, but for You alone, by whom the merits of every man are weighed.

Wherefore, Lord, I account it a great benefit not to have many gifts from which, outwardly and after man's judgment, compliments and praise should follow. And more, it seems to me that, although a man consider and behold his own poverty and the meanness of his own person, he ought not to grieve over it or be sad or dejected, but to conceive great gladness of soul, for You have chosen and daily choose poor humble persons, and such as are despised by the world, to be Your familiar friends and household servants. Witness Your Apostles, whom You made princes of all the world, who nevertheless were well acquainted with the people without complaining or grumbling, so meek and simple without all malice and deceit, that they rejoiced to suffer reproofs for Your Name, in so far that they coveted with great desire even such things as the world abhors and flees.

Thus it appears that there ought to be nothing to

comfort and gladden Your lover and him who has received Your benefits so much as that Your will and pleasure be fulfilled in him after Your eternal disposition for him from the beginning. And he ought to be so well content and so pleased with this that he would gladly be considered the least, as others would be considered the greatest; and he would be as much at peace and as well pleased in the lowest place as in the highest, and as glad to be despised and abject and of no name and reputation in the world, as others to be nobler or greater. Your will, Lord, and the honor of Your Name ought to excel all things, and they ought to please and comfort Your lover more than all other benefits that could be given him.

23. Of Four Things That Bring Peace to the Soul

My son, now I shall teach you the truest way of peace and of perfect liberty.

O Lord Jesus, do as You say, for it is very joyous for me to hear.

Study, my son, to fulfill another man's will rather than your own. Choose always to have little worldly riches rather than much. Seek, also, the lowest place, and desire to be under others rather than above them; desire always and pray that the will of God be wholly done in you. Lo, such a person enters surely into the very true way of peace and inward quiet.

O Lord, this short lesson You have taught me contains in itself much high perfection. It is short in words, but it is full of wisdom and fruitful in virtue. If I observed it well and faithfully, disquiet would not so easily spring up in me as it has.

For, as often as I feel myself restless and discontent, I find that I have departed from this lesson and from this good doctrine. But You, Lord Jesus, who have all things under Your governance, and who always love the health of man's soul, increase Your grace in me still more, so that I may from now on fulfill these teachings and always do what will be to Your honor and to the salvation of my soul.

A Prayer against Evil Thoughts

My Lord Jesus, I beseech You, do not be far from me, but come quickly and help me, for vain thoughts have risen in my heart and worldly fears have troubled me sorely. How shall I break them down? How shall I go unhurt without Your help?

I shall go before you, says our Lord; I shall drive away the pride of your heart; then shall I set open to you the gates of spiritual knowledge and show you the privacy of my secrets.

O Lord, do as You say, and then all wicked imaginings shall flee away from me. Truly, this is my hope and my only comfort—to fly to You in every trouble, to trust steadfastly in You, to call inwardly upon You, and to abide patiently Your coming and Your heavenly consolations which, I trust, will quickly come to me.

A Prayer for the Clearing of Man's Mind

Enlighten me, Lord Jesus, with the clarity of everlasting light, and drive out of my heart all manner of darkness and all vain imaginations and violent temptation. Fight strongly for me and drive away the evil beasts —that is, all my evil and wicked concupiscences—so that peace of conscience may enter and fully rule within me, and that an abundance of glory and praise of Your Name may sound continually in the chamber of my soul in a pure and clean conscience. Command the winds and the tempests of pride to cease; bid the sea of worldly covetousness to be at rest; and charge the northern wind

—that is, the devil's temptation—not to blow. Then great tranquility and peace will be within me.

Send out Your light and Your truth of spiritual knowledge, that it may shine upon the earth, barren and dry. Send down Your grace from above, and with it anoint my dry heart. Give me the water of inward devotion to moisten the dryness of my soul, that it may bring forth good fruit, agreeable and pleasant to You. Raise up my mind that is sore oppressed by the heavy burden of sin, and lift up my desire to the love of spiritual things, so that by a taste of heavenly joy it may loathe to think on any earthly thing. Take me, Lord, and deliver me from the consolation of any earthly creatures which must of necessity shortly perish and fail, for there is nothing created that can fully satisfy my desires. Make me one with You in a sure bond of heavenly love, for You alone are sufficient to Your lover, and without You all things are vain and of no substance.

24. *That It Is Not Good to Search Another Man's Life Inquisitively*

My son, says our Lord, beware against prying into another man's life, and against busying yourself with things that do not concern you. What is this or that to you? Follow Me! What is it to you whether this man is good or bad, or whether he says or does this or that? You do not answer for another man's deeds, but you must indeed make answer for your own. Why, then, do you meddle where it does not concern you? I see and know every man, and I see and behold everything under the sun—how it is with every person, how he thinks, what he wills, to what end his work is directed—all are open to Me, and therefore all things are to be referred to Me. Keep yourself always in good peace, and allow him who will always pry into another man's life to be as busy as he will. And in the end judgment will fall upon a man according to his deeds and words, for he cannot deceive Me, whoever he be.

If you admonish any person for the health of his soul, be careful not to do it to win for yourself name or fame in the world. Be careful not to have the too-familiar or private love of any person, for such things cause great disquiet of mind, and will make you also lose the reward you should have from God, and will bring great darkness into your soul. I would gladly speak to you My words, and open to you the secret mysteries of fraternal correction, if you would prepare your soul for My coming and would open your heart faithfully to Me. Have foresight, wake diligently in prayer, humble yourself in everything, and you will find great comfort in God and little resistance from your fellow Christian.

25. *In What Things Peace of Heart and the Greatest Profit of Man Rest*

My son, says our Lord Jesus, I have said to My disciples, My peace I leave you, My peace I give you; not as the world gives, but much more than it can give. All men desire peace, but all will not do what pertains to peace. My peace is with the humble and gentle in heart, and your peace will be in much patience. If you will hear Me and follow My words, you will have a great plenty of peace.

O Lord, what shall I do to come to that peace?

You shall in all your works take good heed what you do and say, and you shall set your whole intention to please Me, and you shall desire and seek nothing without Me, and you shall not judge presumptiously of other men's deeds, nor shall you meddle with things that do not pertain to you. If you do this, it may be that you will be little or seldom troubled. Still, never to feel any manner of trouble or suffer any weariness in body or soul is not the condition of this life, but of the life to come.

Do not think, therefore, that you have found true peace when you feel no grief, or that all is well with you when you have no adversary, or that all is perfect when everything happens as you desire, or even that you are great in God's sight or especially loved by Him because you have great fervor in devotion and great sweetness in contemplation. A true lover of virtue is not known by these things, and the true perfection of man does not stand in them.

In what, then, Lord, does true perfection stand?

It stands in a man offering all his heart wholly to God, not seeking himself or his own will, either in great things or in small, in time or in eternity, but abiding always unchanged and always yielding to God equal thanks for things pleasing and displeasing, weighing them all in one same balance, as in His love. And if he is so strong in God that when inward consolation is withdrawn he stirs his heart to suffer more, if God so will, yet does not justify himself or praise himself as holy and righteous, then he walks in the very true way of peace, and may well have a sure and perfect hope that he will see Me face to face in everlasting joy in the kingdom of heaven. And if he can come to a perfect and full contempt and despising of himself, then he will have a full abundance of rest and peace in joy everlasting, according to the measure of his gift.

26. *Of the Liberty, Excellence, and Worthiness of a Free Mind*

Lord, it is the work of a perfect man never to isolate his mind from a consideration of heavenly things, and to carry on among many cares as if he were without care, not in the manner of an idle or a dissolute person, but by the special prerogative of a free mind always busy in God's service, not clinging to any creature by inordinate affection.

I beseech You, therefore, my Lord Jesus, most meek and merciful, to keep me from the busyness and cares of the world so that I may not be overmuch disquieted by the necessities of bodily nature, nor captured by the voluptuous pleasures of the world and of the flesh. In like manner, may You preserve me from all hindrance of the soul, so that I may not be broken by excessive sadness, sorrow, or worldly fear. By these prayers I ask not only to be delivered from such vanities as the world craves, but also from such miseries as grieve my soul, burdened by the common malediction of mankind, that is, by the corruption of the bodily senses, by which I am so grieved and hindered that I cannot have liberty of spirit to behold You when I would.

O Lord God, who are sweetness unspeakable, turn all fleshly delight into bitterness to me, delights which would turn me from the love of eternal things to the love of short and unworthy sensible pleasure. Do not let flesh and blood overcome me, or the world with its short glory deceive me, or the devil, with his thousandfold arts, ensnare me, but give me spiritual strength to resist, patience to suffer, and constancy to persevere. In place of all worldly consolation, give me the most sweet consolation of the Holy Spirit, and in place of all fleshly love send into my soul the love of Your holy Name.

Behold—meat, drink, clothing, and all other necessities of the body are painful and troublesome to a fervent spirit which, if it might, would always rest in God and in spiritual things. Grant me, therefore, grace to use such bodily necessities temperately, and grace not to be deceived by excessive desire for them. It is not lawful to forsake all things, for physical nature must be preserved, and Your holy law prohibits superfluous things to be sought more for pleasure than for necessity, for so the flesh would rebel against the spirit. Wherefore, Lord, I beseech You, that the hand of Your grace may so govern and teach me that I shall not exceed by any manner of superfluity.

27. *That Private Love Most Withholds a Man from God*

My son, says our Lord, it behooves you to give all for all, and to keep nothing of your own love, for love of yourself hurts you more than any other thing in this world. According to your love and your affection, everything more or less cleaves to you. If your love is pure, simple and well ordered, you will be without inordinate affection for any creature. Desire nothing it is not lawful for you to have, and have nothing that can hinder you from spiritual work or that may take from you inward liberty of soul. It is a marvel that you do not fully commit yourself to Me with all your heart, with all you can have or desire. Why are you thus consumed with vain sorrow? Why are you weary with superfluous cares? Stand ready to My will, and you will find nothing to hurt or hinder you. But if you seek this thing or that, or would be in this place or that place for your own profit and your own pleasure, you will never be at rest, and you will never be free from some trouble of mind; in every place, something you dislike will be found.

When transitory things are possessed and greatly multiplied in the world, they do not always help a man's soul to peace. But they help, rather, when they are despised and fully cut away from the love and desire of the heart. And this is to be understood not only of gold and silver and other worldly riches, but also of the desire for honor and praise in the world, which shortly vanish and pass away as smoke upon the wind.

Place helps little if the spirit of fervor is absent, and

the peace a man gains outwardly will not long stand whole if it lacks true inward peace of heart. Though you change your place, it will improve you little unless you stand firm and steadfast in Me. For by new occasions that daily arise you will find the very things from which you fled, and perhaps they will be much more perilous and much more harmful than the first were.

A Prayer for the Purifying of Man's Soul and to Obtain Heavenly Wisdom and the Grace of God

Confirm me, Lord, by the grace of the Holy Spirit, and give me grace to be strong inwardly in soul and to cast out from it all unprofitable business of the world and of the flesh, that it may not be led by unstable desires of earthly things. And grant that I may behold all things in this world as they are—transitory and of short abiding, and I myself also to pass away together with them, for nothing under the sun can long abide, but all is vanity and affliction of spirit. Oh, how wise is he who feels and understands what I have said to be true.

Therefore, O Lord, give me true heavenly wisdom, that I may learn to seek You and to find You, and above all things to love You, and to understand and know all other things as they are, after the direction of Your wisdom, and not otherwise. And give me grace, also, to withdraw myself from those who flatter me, and patiently to tolerate those who grieve me. It is great wisdom not to be moved by every blast of words, nor to give ear to him who flatters, as it were, with the song of the sirens. The way so begun will bring him who walks it to a good and blessed ending.

28. Against the Evil Saying of Detractors

My son, says our Saviour Christ, you will not take it to heart, though some people think or say of you evil that you would gladly not hear, for you will think even worse of yourself, and that no man is as evil as you. If you are well ordered in your soul, you will not care much for such flying words. It is no little wisdom for a man to keep himself in silence and in good peace when evil words are spoken to him, and to turn his heart to God and not to be troubled with man's judgment.

Do not let your peace depend on the hearts of men; whatever they say about you, good or bad, you are not because of it another man, for as you are, you are. Where is true peace and true glory? Is it not in Me? Yes, truly. Therefore, he who neither desires to please men nor fears to displease them will have great plenty of peace; for all disquiet of heart and restlessness of mind come from inordinate love and groundless fear.

29. How Almighty God Is to be Called upon in Time of Tribulation

Lord, may Your Name be blessed forever, who will that this temptation and tribulation fall upon me. I may not escape it, but, of necessity, I am driven to flee to You, that You may deign to help me and to turn all to my spiritual progress.

O Lord, I am in trouble, and it is not well with me, for I am greatly vexed by this present suffering. I am caught in anguish and trouble on every side, yet I know that I am come to this hour so that You may be praised when I am made perfectly humble before You and glorified when I am clearly freed through Your grace. O most beloved Father, may it be pleasing to You to deliver me, for what can I do, most sinful wretch, or where can I go without You? O Lord, give me patience in all my afflictions. Help me, O Lord God, and I will not fear or dread whatever troubles befall me.

And now what shall I say, save that Your will be done in me? I have deserved to be troubled and grieved, and therefore it is fitting that I should suffer so long as it will please You. Would to God that I might endure patiently, until the furious tempests pass and peace of heart comes again. Your mighty hand, Lord, is strong enough to take this trouble from me, and to make its cruel assaults gentle, as You have oftentimes done before, so that I will not utterly fail. The harder it is to me, the lighter it is to You, and when I am clearly delivered by You, then shall I say: This is the change of the right hand of the Almighty, that is, the Blessed Trinity, to whom be joy, honor, and glory everlastingly.

30. Of the Help of God to be Asked, and of a Full Trust to Recover Our Former Grace through Devout Prayer

My son, I am the Lord who sends comfort in time of tribulation. Come, therefore, to Me when it is not well with you. What hinders you most is that you turn yourself to Me too slowly; before you pray heartily to Me you seek many other comforts, and refresh your spirit in outward things. And so it comes about that all that you do helps you little, until you can behold and see that I am He who sends comfort to all who faithfully call to Me, and that without Me there can be no profitable counsel or perfect remedy.

But now, take good spirit. After your trouble, be comforted in Me, and have full trust in the light of My mercy, for I am near you to help and restore you, not only to the same grace you had at first, but to more grace in great abundance. Is there anything hard or impossible to Me, or am I like a man who says a thing and does not do it? Where is your faith? Stand strongly and perseveringly in Me; be steadfast, awaiting My promise; and you will have comfort when it will be most expedient to you. Abide, abide and wait for Me, and I will come soon to you and help you.

It is temptation that troubles you, and a vague dread that makes you fear. But of what avail is such fear or dread of things that perhaps will never come, save that the spiritual enemy desires that you should have sorrow upon sorrow. Bear your present troubles patiently, therefore, and do not fear overmuch those that are to come, for sufficient to the day is the day's evil. It is vain and unprofitable to be sad or glad for things which perhaps will never happen or come. But it is the instability of man that he will be deceived and will so easily follow the suggestion of the enemy, who does not care whether he deceives by true or false suggestion, nor whether he deceives by love of things present or by fear of things to come. Therefore, do not be troubled and do not fear. Trust strongly in Me and have perfect hope in My mercy. When you think you are very far from Me, I am often quite close to you; when you think all is lost, then the greater reward often follows. All is not lost, though some things happen contrary to your will. You should not judge of them according to your outward feeling, nor should you take any grief so sorely to heart that you do not have good hope to escape it. You should not think yourself wholly forsaken by Me, though I send you for a time some grief and trouble, for this is the surer way to the kingdom of heaven.

Doubtless, it is more expedient to you and to My other servants sometimes to be proved by adversity than always to have all things according to your will. I know the hidden features of man, and that it is much more expedient to the health of his soul to be left sometimes to himself without spiritual sweetness or comfort, lest, perhaps, he be raised up by pride, and think himself better than he is. What I have given I may take away, and may restore it again when it pleases Me. When I give something to any person, what I have given is My own, and when I take it away again, I take nothing of his, for every good gift, every perfect reward, comes from Me. If I send you trouble or heaviness, in what way soever, take it gladly and do not despise it, and do not let your heart fail you in the trouble, for I may soon lift you up again, and turn your heaviness into great joy and spiritual gladness, and truly I am just and much to be glorified and praised when I act so with you.

If you understand properly and behold yourself truly as you are, you will never be so immediately grieved because of any adversity; rather, you will find joy in it, and think it the greatest gift that I do not abstain from scourging you with such trouble and adversity. I said to My disciples: As My Father loves Me, so I love you, and yet I sent them forth into the world not to have temporal joy, but to meet great battles; not to have honors, but injuries; not to be idle, but to labor; not to rest, but to bring forth much good fruit in patience and in good works. My son, remember well these words I have spoken to you, for they are true and cannot be denied.

31. How We Should Forget All Created Things, That We May Find Our Creator

Lord, I have great need of Your grace, of Your great singular grace, before I arrive where no creature will hinder me from perfect contemplation of You. As long as any transitory thing holds me or rules within me, I cannot fly freely to You. He desires to fly without hindrance who says: Who shall give me wings like the dove, that I may fly into the bosom of my Saviour and into the place of His blessed wounds, and rest there?

I see well that no man is more at rest in this world than he who always has his mind and his whole intention directed upward to God, and desires nothing from the world. It behooves him, therefore, who would perfectly forsake himself and behold You, to rise above all creatures and himself, also, and through elevation of mind to see and behold that You, Maker of all things, have nothing like to Yourself among all creatures. Unless a man is clearly delivered from all love of creatures, he cannot fully attend to his Creator; this is the chief reason why there are so few contemplatives—that is to say, because there are so few who will willingly set themselves apart from the love of created things. Great grace is required for contemplation, for it lifts up the soul and ravishes it in spirit above itself. Unless a man is lifted up in spirit above himself and is in his love completely freed from all creatures and perfectly and fully united to God, whatever else he knows or has, whether it be virtue or learning, will be worth little before God. Therefore, he who accounts anything great or worthy to be praised, save God alone, will have but little virtue and will long lie bound to earthly things. All other things besides God are nothing, and are to be accounted as nothing. There is a great difference between the wisdom of a devout man, enlightened by grace, and the learning of a subtle and studious scholar; that learning which comes by the influence and gracious gift of God is much more noble and worthy than that learning which is gained by the labor and study of man.

Many desire to have the gift of contemplation, but they will not use such means as are required for contemplation. One great hindrance to contemplation is that we rely so much on outward signs and material things and pay no heed to the spirit. I do not know how it is, or by what spirit we are led, or what we pretend, we who are called spiritual persons, that we devote greater study and labor to transitory things than we do to know the inward state of our own soul. But alas, for sorrow, as soon as we have given a short moment of recollection to God, we turn to pursue outward things, and do not search our own conscience with due examination, as we should, or heed where our affection rests or have sorrow that our deeds are as evil and as unclean as they are. The people corrupted themselves by fleshly uncleanness, and therefore the great flood followed; truly, when our inward affection is corrupt, it must needs be that our deeds which follow are also corrupt, for from a clean heart springs the fruit of a good life.

It is often asked what deeds such a man has done, but there is little regard for the zeal and intention with which he did them. Whether a man is rich, strong, fair, able, a good writer, a good singer, or a good laboror is often asked; but how poor he is in spirit, how patient and humble, how devout, and how inwardly turned to God are little regarded. Nature beholds the outward deed, but grace turns itself to the inward intention of the deed. The first is often deceived, but the second puts its trust wholly in God, and is not deceived.

32. *How We Should Forsake Ourselves, and Thrust All Covetousness out of Our Hearts*

My son, says our Lord, you will not have perfect liberty of mind unless you wholly forsake yourself. All possessors of worldly goods and all lovers of themselves, all covetous persons, all curious, all vain-glorious, all who gad about, all who pursue the transitory things of this world, greedily seeking those that will not long endure, and not the things of Jesus Christ, are as men fettered and bound with chains. They have no perfect liberty, or freedom of spirit, for all things not wrought by God will perish. Hold well in your mind this brief word: Forsake all things, and you will find all things. Forsake coveting, and you will find great rest. Print well in your mind what I have said, for when you have fulfilled it, you will know well that it is true.

Lord, this lesson is not one day's work, or play for children—in it is contained the full perfection of all religion.

My son, you ought not to be turned from God, or to be in any way discouraged in His service, when you hear of the life of perfect men; rather, you ought to be stirred thereby to greater perfection, and at least to a desire in your heart to arrive at it. But would to God that you were first come to this point, that you were not a lover of yourself, but that you would keep My commandments, and the commandments of him whom I have appointed to be your spiritual father, for then you would please Me greatly, and then all your life would pass in joy and peace. You have yet many things to renounce; unless you can wholly forsake them, you will not get what you desire. Therefore, I counsel you to buy from Me bright, shining gold—that is, heavenly wisdom which despises all earthly things. Cast away from yourself all worldly wisdom, all man's comfort, and all your own affections, and choose to have things abject rather than things precious and significant in the sight of the world.

True heavenly wisdom seems to many to be mean and little, and is well-nigh forgotten. Many can say with their mouth that it is good not to desire to be magnified in the world, but their life does not follow their speech, and it therefore is seen that they desire worldly glory secretly in their heart. Yet this is a precious pearl and high virtue that is hid from many people because of their presumption. Let him who can obtain it do so.

33. Of the Instability of Man's Heart, and That Our Full Intent in All Things Should be toward God

My son, look that you do not believe your own affection, for it often changes from one to another. As long as you live, you will be subject to change, whether you will it or not—now glad, now sorrowful; now pleased, now displeased; now devout, now undevout; now vigorous, now slothful; now gloomy, now merry.

But a wise man who is well taught in spiritual labor stands unshaken in all such things, and heeds little what he feels, or from what side the wind of instability blows. All the intention and study of his mind is how he can most profit in virtue to the most fruitful and blessed end. By such a full intention wholly directed to God a man may abide steadfast and unshaken in himself among many adversities, and the more pure and clean his intention is, the more firm will he be in every storm.

But alas, for sorrow, the eye of a man's soul is soon darkened, for it easily beholds pleasant things that come from the world and from the flesh, insomuch that there is seldom found any person who is free and clear from the poisonous desire to hear tales or some other fantasy, and that of his own seeking. In such manner the people came to Bethany to Martha and to Mary Magdalene, not for the love of our Lord Jesus, but to see Lazarus, whom He had raised from death to life. Wherefore, the eye of the soul is to be kept wholly bright, that it may always be pure and clean, and that above all passing things it may be wholly directed to God. May God grant us this.

34. How Sweet Our Lord God Tastes to His Lover above All Things and in All Things

Our Lord God is to me all in all. Since He is, what more would I have and what more can I desire? Oh, this is a delicious and a sweet word, to say that our Lord is to me all in all, but it is so to Him who loves the Word and not the world.

Enough is said to him who understands; yet it is pleasing to him who loves to repeat it often. I may, therefore, speak more plainly of this matter and say: Lord, when You are present to me, all things are pleasant and agreeable; when You are absent, all things are irksome and most unpleasant. When You come, You put my heart at rest, and bring into it a new joy. You make Your lover feel and understand the truth, and have true judgment in all things, and in all things to glorify and praise You. O Lord, without You nothing can long be agreeable or pleasant, for if anything is pleasant or sweet it must be through the help of Your grace, and it must be seasoned with the spice of Your wisdom.

What will not be sweet to him to whom You are the greatest sweetness? And what can be joyous or pleasant to him who finds no sweetness in You? The worldly wise and those who taste earthly delights fail in this wisdom, for in worldly wisdom is found great vanity, and in fleshly pleasures everlasting death. Therefore, those who follow You, Lord, by despising the world and by perfect mortification of their fleshly desires, are known to be very wise, for they are led from vanity to truth and from fleshly pleasure to spiritual purity. God tastes wonderfully sweet to such persons, and they refer whatever they find in created things to the glory and praise of their Creator. They see well that there is a great difference between the creature and the Creator, between time and eternity, between light created and Light uncreated.

O everlasting Light, far surpassing all created things, send down the beams of Your brightness from above, and purify, gladden, and illuminate in me all the inward corners of my heart. Quicken my spirit with all its powers, that it may cleave fast and be joined to You in joyful gladness of spiritual rapture. Oh, when will that blessed hour come when You will visit me and gladden me with Your blessed presence, so that You are to me all in all. As long as that gift is not given me, there will be in me no full joy.

But alas, for sorrow, my old nature—that is, my earthly affection—still lives in me, and is not yet fully crucified or perfectly dead. The flesh still strives strongly against the spirit and stirs up great inward battle against me, and does not allow the kingdom of my soul to live in peace.

But You, good Lord, who have lordship over the power of the sea, and calm the streams of its flowing, arise and help me! Break down the power of my enemy, which always stirs up this battle within me. Show the strength of Your goodness, and let the power of Your right hand be glorified in me, for there is for me no other hope or refuge save in You only, my Lord, my God, to whom be joy, glory, and honor, everlastingly.

35. *That There Is No Complete Security from Temptation in This Life*

Our Lord says to His servant: You will never be safe from temptation and tribulation in this life, and therefore spiritual armor is necessary for you as long as you live. You are among your enemies and will be troubled and vexed by them on every side; unless you use everywhere the shield of patience, you will not long preserve yourself unwounded. And more than that—if you do not set your heart strongly upon Me, with a ready will to suffer all things patiently for Me, you cannot long bear this struggle, or come to the reward of the blessed saints. It behooves you, therefore, resolutely to forego many things and to use a strong hand against all the assaults of the enemy. To him who overcomes is promised the food of angels; to him who is overcome is left much misery.

If you seek rest in this life, how will you, then, come to everlasting rest? Do not determine to have rest here, but to have patience, and seek true rest not on earth, but in heaven; not in man or in any creature, but in God alone, where true rest is. You ought gladly to suffer all things for the love of God: all labors, sorrows, temptations, vexations; all anguish, need, sickness, injuries, evil sayings, reproaches; all oppressions, confusions, corrections, and despisings. These greatly help a man to virtue; these prove the true knight of Christ and prepare for him a heavenly crown. And I shall reward him with everlasting reward for his short labor, with infinite glory for his transitory confusion.

Do you believe that you will always have spiritual comfort after your own will? No, no; My saints did not have such spiritual comfort. They had many great griefs and various temptations and great desolation, but they bore all with patience, and trusted more in Me than in themselves, for they knew well that the sufferings of this world cannot of themselves merit the glory that is ordained for them in the kingdom of heaven. Would you expect to have immediately what others before you could scarcely obtain after great weeping and labor?

Await patiently the coming of our Lord. Do His bidding manfully, be comforted in Him, and do not mistrust Him. Do not quit His service because of suffering or fear, but expose your body and soul constantly in His honor, in all good physical and spiritual toil, and He will reward you most fully for your good work, and will be with you and help you in every trouble that may befall you. So may it be.

36. *Against the Vain Judgments of Men*

My son, fix your heart steadfastly in God, and do not fear the judgments of men, where your own conscience witnesses that you are innocent and pure. It is very good and blessed sometimes to suffer such sayings, and it will not be irksome to a humble heart which trusts more in God than in itself. People often speak much, yet little faith is to be put in their sayings. It is not possible to please all men, for, though St. Paul labored as much as he might to please all people in God and did for all men all he could for their salvation, he nevertheless could not prevent himself from being judged by others and despised by them. And so he committed all to God, who knows all things, and armed himself with patience and humility against all things that could be untruly spoken against him. Nevertheless, he sometimes answered to the charges, lest, by his silence, hurt or hindrance might have risen for others.

What are you, then, who dread a mortal man so deeply? Today he is, and tomorrow he does not appear. Fear God, and you will not need to fear man. What can man do to you in words or injuries? He hurts himself more than he hurts you, and in the end, whoever he be, he will not escape the judgment of God. Have God always before the eye of your soul, and do not answer to the charge in many words. If you seem for a time to suffer confusion that you have not deserved, do not count it as little, and do not, through impatience, diminish your reward. Rather, lift up your heart to God in heaven, for He is able to deliver you from all confusion and wrong and to reward every man as he deserves, and much more than he can deserve.

37. Of a Pure and a Complete Forsaking of Ourselves and of Our Own Will, So That We May Obtain Freedom of Spirit and Follow the Will of God

My son, says our Lord, forsake yourself, and you will find Me. Stand without choice, without following your own will, and without all possessions, and you will advance much in grace. If you resign yourself wholly into my hands, and take back nothing for yourself, you will have more grace from Me.

O Lord, how often should I resign myself to you, and in what things should I forsake myself?

Always and in every hour, in great things and in small things; I except nothing. In all things I would find you naked and poor, and bereft of your own will. How can you be Mine, and I yours, unless you are clearly deprived of your own will within and without? And the sooner you can bring this about, the sooner will it be better with you, and the more fully and clearly you can do it, the more fully you will please Me and the more will you win.

Some people resign themselves to Me, but with some reservation, for they do not fully trust Me, and therefore study to provide for themselves; and some at the beginning offer all to Me, but afterwards, when any temptation comes, they turn again to their own will and to what they promised to forsake, and therefore they gain little in virtue. Truly, such persons will never come to perfect cleanness and freedom of heart, or to the grace of familiarity with Me, save through a complete, perfect forsaking of themselves and a daily offering of themselves and all that is theirs completely to Me. Without that, no man can have perfect fruition and be made one with Me.

I have said to you many times before, and I say to you yet again, forsake yourself and resign yourself wholly to Me, and you will have great inward peace. Give all for all, and keep nothing to yourself after your own will. Stand purely and firmly in Me, and you will have Me, and will be so pure in heart and in soul that darkness of conscience or slavery to sin will never have power in you. Endeavor, therefore, to gain this freedom of spirit of which I speak. Pray for it, study for it and always desire it in your heart—that is to say, that you may clearly be deprived and bereft of all possessions and of your own will, and that, stripped of all worldly things, you may follow Me, who hung naked for you upon the cross, and that in your love you may die to yourself and to all worldly things, and blessedly live to Me. Then, if you do so, all vanities and all imaginings and all superfluous cares of the world and of the flesh will fail and fade and pass away. Then, also, immoderate fear and inordinate love will die in you, and you will blessedly live in Me, and I in you.

38. How a Man Should Rule Himself in Outward Things, and How He Ought to Call on God for Help in All Perils and Dangers

Our Lord Jesus says to His servant: You ought diligently to take heed that in every place, in every deed, and in every outward occupation you may be inwardly free in your soul and rule over yourself. Let all things be subject to you as in your love, and not you subject to them; be lord and governor over your deeds, not a servant or a slave; rather, be free as a true Hebrew—that is to say, as a true Christian man, entering into the number and freedom of the children of God, who stand upon present things and look toward everlasting things, and behold things transitory on one side, and things everlasting upon the other. Such are not drawn down to the love of worldly goods; rather, they draw worldly goods to serve in such manner as they are ordained by God, and as they are instituted to do by the high Maker of all things, who leaves nothing inordinate in His creatures.

If, in any perils and doubt, you do not stand according to the outward appearance, but if, in every such doubt, you enter into your soul by prayer, as Moses went into the tabernacle to ask counsel of God, you will soon hear the answer of our Lord which will instruct you sufficiently in many things, both present and to come. We read that Moses always had recourse to the tabernacle of God when doubts and questions were to be solved, and that he there asked the help of God through devout prayers, in his own perils and dangers as well as in those of the people. So should you enter into the secret tabernacle of your own heart, and there ask inwardly, with good devotion, the help of God in all such doubts and perils. We read that Joshua and the children of Israel were deceived by the Gibeonites because they gave easy credence to their sayings and did not first ask counsel of God, as they should have done. And so, by the fair words of the Gibeonites and through a false pity, Joshua and the children of Israel were deluded and greatly deceived.

39. *That a Man Should Not Be Importunate in His Business*

My son, says our Lord, always commit your cause to Me, and I shall dispose of it well for you, when the time comes. Await My ordinance and direction, and you will find great profit and help in them.

O Lord, I will gladly commit all things to You, for there is little that I can do for myself. Would to God that I did not cling to desire of worldly things, but that

I might always offer myself wholly to Your will and pleasure.

My son, it is good for you to do so. Sometimes, a man who trusts in himself and his own will sets his mind much to bring this or that about as he desires. But when he has attained what he desires, than he begins to feel quite differently toward it than he did before. The affections and desires of man are not always constant, but drive a man often from one thing to another. Therefore, it is no small thing for a man fully to forsake himself, though it be in very little and small things.

Truly, the very perfection of man is a perfect denying and a complete forsaking of himself; such a man is very free and beloved of God. But the old ancient enemy, the devil, who resists goodness all he can, does not long cease from tempting. Night and day he makes grievous assaults to see whether he can catch any unwary person in his snare of deceit. Therefore, watch and pray, that you be not deceived by temptation.

40. *That a Man Has No Goodness of Himself, and That He May Not Rightfully Glorify Himself in Anything*

O Lord, what is man, that You deign to regard him? What has he done for You, that You will visit him with Your grace, and how can he complain if You sometimes forsake him? What can I justly say, even though You do not grant me what I ask? Truly, I can well think and say: I am nothing and I have no goodness of myself, but in all things I am of myself insufficient and tend to nothing. Unless You help me and inwardly instruct and teach me, I will be wholly slothful and unprofitable in every way. O Lord, You are always the same, and ever shall be the same—always good, always righteous and holy—and You justly and blessedly dispose all things according to Your wisdom. But I, wretched one, who am always more ready and prone to evil than to good, do not always abide the same, for I change seven times a day. Nevertheless, it will be better with me when it will please You to put forth Your helping hand; for You only, without man, can help me and so confirm and strengthen me that my heart will not so lightly be changed, but shall be wholly fixed and finally rest in You.

Truly, if I could cast away from myself all man's comfort, either for devotion, or because I am compelled to it by necessity, since I find no comfort in man, then I might trust well in Your grace to have from You new visitation and new heavenly consolation.

But I confess it as true that I am not worthy to have any such consolation, and I thank You, as often as any good thing comes to me, for all that is good comes from You. I am but vanity and naught and an unconstant and feeble man before You. In what, therefore, can I justly glorify myself, and why should I look to be thought great? Truly, vainglory is a perilous sickness, a grievous pestilence, and a very great vanity, for it draws a man away from the true joy he should have in God and robs him of all heavenly grace. When a man pleases himself, he displeases You, and when he delights in the praise of man, he is deprived of true virtue, for true, steadfast gladness is to rejoice in You, and not in himself, in Your Name, and not in his own virtue or in any creature. Therefore, may Your Name and not mine be praised, your works and not mine magnified, your goodness always blessed, so that nothing of man's praise and honor be given to me.

You are my glory and the joy of my heart. In You shall I be glorified, and in You always shall I rejoice. For myself, I shall glory in nothing but in my infirmities. Let the nations seek glory among themselves, but I will seek none, save only that which is from You. All man's glory, all temporal honor, and all worldly position are but foolishness and vanity, compared to Your eternal glory.

O Truth, O Mercy, O Blessed Trinity, to You be praise, glory, and honor, everlastingly.

41. How All Temporal Honor Is to be Despised

My son, do not be grieved, though you see other men honored and exalted, and yourself despised and set at naught. If you raise up your heart to Me in heaven, the malice of man on earth will grieve you little.

O Lord, we are here in great darkness and soon deceived by vanity; but, truly, if I regarded myself well, I would clearly see that no creature had ever done me wrong and that therefore I have nothing of which I may justly complain. But, inasmuch as I have often sinned and grievously offended You, all creatures are therefore armed against me. Confusion and contempt, therefore, are due me, but praise, honor and glory are Your due. Unless I can bring myself to this point—that I would gladly be forsaken and seem as nothing in the world—I cannot inwardly be at peace, or grounded upon You, or spiritually illuminated, or yet fully one with You.

42. That Our Trust Is Not to be Put in Worldly People

My son, if, for your own pleasure or worldly friendship, you set your peace in any person, you will always be unstable, and you will never be content. But if you always have recourse to Truth everlasting, that is, God Himself, then the death or the departure of your dearest friend, whoever he be, will grieve you little. The love of your friend ought always to be referred to Me, and he is to be loved for Me, no matter how good or profitable he seems to you in this life. Without Me, friendship is worth nothing and cannot long endure; nor is that love true and clean that is not knit by Me. You ought, therefore, to be so mortified to all such affection for worldly men that, as much as you can, you would desire to be without all man's comfort.

A man draws nearer to God in so far as he can withdraw himself from the world and from all worldly comfort, and he ascends higher toward God in so far as he can descend lower in himself and becomes mean and abject in his own sight. He who ascribes any goodness to himself withstands the grace of God and hinders it from living within him, for the grace of the Holy Spirit always seeks a meek and a humble heart. If you could bring yourself to nothing, and wholly banish from your heart all created love, then, says our Lord, I should come to you with great abundance of My grace. But when you look to created things, then the sight of your Creator is justly withdrawn from you. Learn, therefore, to overcome yourself for the love of Him who made you like Himself, and you will soon come to great spiritual knowledge. However little the thing a man loves, if he loves it inordinately, it hinders him greatly from the true and perfect love he should have for God.

43. *That We Should Disdain Vain Secular Learning*

My son, says our Lord, do not let fair and subtle words move you, for the kingdom of heaven does not stand in words, but in good, virtuous works. Give heed to My words, for they enflame the heart and enlighten the understanding; they bring compunction of heart for sins past, and oftentimes cause great heavenly comfort to come into the soul. Never read in any science to the end that you may be called wise. Study, rather, to mortify in yourself, as much as possible, all stirring of sin; that will be more profitable to you than the knowledge of many hard or subtle questions. Even when you have read and understood many puzzling things it nevertheless behooves you to come to One who is the Beginning of all things, that is, God Himself; otherwise, your knowledge will avail you little.

I am He who teaches a man wisdom and gives more understanding to humble persons than can be given by man's teaching. And he to whom I speak will soon become wise and will advance much in spirit, but pain and woe will be to those who seek only for curious learning, taking little heed of the way to serve God. The time will come when Christ, Lord of angels and Master of all masters, will appear to hear the lesson of every creature and to examine the conscience of every person. And then will Jerusalem, that is, every man's soul, be searched with lanterns and lights of God's high knowledge and just judgments. Then, also, will the deeds and thoughts of every man be revealed and all excuses and all vain arguments will fail.

I am He who also suddenly illuminates and lifts up a humble soul, so that it can take and receive in short time the true reason of the wisdom of God more perfectly than another who studies ten years in the schools and lacks humility. I teach without sound of words, without diversity of opinions, without desire for honor, and without strife and arguments. I am He who teaches all the people to despise earthly things, to loathe things that are present, to seek and savor eternal things, to flee honors, to bear patiently all evil words, to put their trust wholly in Me, to desire nothing without Me, and above all things fervently to love Me.

Through the interior love they had for me some men learned many great things and spoke of the high mysteries of my Godhead. They profit more in forsaking all things than in studying for high and subtle learning. To some men I speak ordinary things; to some, special things. To some I appear sweetly in signs and symbols; to some I give great understanding of Scripture and open to them high, secret mysteries. There are in books the same voice and the same letters read, but they do not instruct all people alike, for I am within, secretly hidden in the letter, the Teacher of truth, the Searcher of man's heart, the Knower of thoughts, the Promoter of good works, and the Rewarder of all men, as My wisdom and goodness judge them to have deserved, and in no other way.

44. That We Should Not Greatly Regard Outward Things, and Consider but Little the Judgment of Man

My son, it is profitable to you to be ignorant in many things and to think of yourself as dead to the world and one to whom all the world is crucified. And you must also, as though your ear were deaf, let many things pass as though you neither heard nor saw them, and think on such things as shall cause you inward peace of soul. It is also more profitable to you to turn the soul from things that displease you, and to let every man hold his opinion in them as seems best to him, rather than to strive against it with ill-considered words. Truly, if you were well established in God and beheld His judgments well, you would easily be content to be judged by others and to be overcome by others as our Lord Jesus was for you at the time of His Passion.

O Lord, since what You say is true, what will become of us who heed worldly things so much, and bewail so greatly a little temporal loss? We labor and run after worldly profit with all our might, but we regard little our spiritual profit and the salvation of our souls. We set much store by things that profit us little or nothing, but we nearly forget what is most necessary to us. All men run gladly to outward things, and truly, unless they sharply turn back, they will gladly rest in them, and in the end, that will be a great peril and danger to them.

45. *That Men Are Not Always to be Believed, Because They So Easily Offend in Words*

Lord, send me help in my troubles, for man's help is worth little. How often have I found no friendship where I thought I should have found it, and how often have I found it where I least presumed it to be? Wherefore, it is a vain thing to trust in man, for the certain trust and help of righteous men is only in You. Be You therefore blessed, Lord, in all things that happen to us, for we are weak and unstable, soon deceived and soon changed from one thing to another.

Who can so cautiously and so assuredly guard himself in everything that he will not sometimes fall into some deceit and some perplexity? Truly, very few. But he who trusts in You and seeks You with a clean heart does not so easily slip away from You. And if he happens to fall into any trouble or perplexity, whatever and how grievous soever it be, he will soon either be delivered by You, or be comforted by You, for You never forsake him who trusts in You. It is very hard to find a friend so faithful and so true that he will persevere with his friend in all his troubles, but You, Lord, are most faithful in all things, and no other can be found like You. Oh, how well did that holy soul relish spiritual things who said: My mind is fixed in God and is fully grounded in Christ. Surely, if it were so with me, the fear of man would not so easily enter into me and other men's words would not so soon move me.

Who can foresee all things or prevent all the evils that are to come? Yet if things foreseen often do great hurt, what will those things do that are not foreseen?

But why have I, wretched one, not better seen to myself? Why have I so easily believed other men's sayings? Truly, because we are men, and indeed but frail men, though we may be esteemed and thought of by many as angels in our deportment. Whom can I believe save only You? You are the Truth that deceives no man and that cannot be deceived. On the other hand, every man is a liar, weak and unstable and slippery, most especially in words, so that what seems openly to be true can scarcely be believed. How prudently, therefore, have You warned us to beware of the levity of man, and that our familiar servants may be our enemies, so that, though one may say: Lo, here is your friend, or there is your friend, it cannot be believed.

I am taught by my own hurt, and would to God it might be a warning to me and not an occasion of greater folly. Someone says to me: Be careful, be careful. Keep what I shall show you to yourself, and when I keep it and believe it to be secret, he cannot keep the secret as he himself desires, but straightway betrays both himself and me and goes his way. From such tales and from such unstable men, Lord, defend me, so that I may not fall into their hands, and never myself commit any such things. Give to my mouth, Lord, a true and steadfast word and drive far from me a deceitful tongue, for I ought to beware not to do to any other what I would not have others do to me.

Oh, how good and how peaceful it is to keep silence about other men's words and deeds, and not to give full credence until the truth be proved, not to report lightly to others all we see or hear, and not to be moved with every bluff of words, to open our heart fully but to very few, to seek You always, who are the Beholder of man's heart, and to desire that all things in us, inwardly and outwardly, may be fulfilled after Your will. How sure a thing it is, too, for the possession of heavenly grace, to flee as far as we can the conversation of all worldly people and not to desire things that seem outwardly to be pleasant and agreeable, but with all the study of our heart to seek such things as bring fervor of spirit and amendment of life. A virtue known and praised in untimely fashion has been truly a great harm to many persons, and, to the contrary, a grace kept in silence and not quickly reported to others has been very profitable to some in this frail life that is full of temptation and secret envy.

46. *That We Must Put All Our Confidence in God, When Evil Words Are Spoken*

My son, says our Lord, stand strongly and trust faithfully in Me. What are words but wind? They fly in the air, but they never hurt a stone on the ground. And if you know that you are not guilty, think that you will gladly suffer such words for God. It is but a little thing for you to suffer sometimes a hasty word, since you are not yet able to suffer hard strokes. But why is it that so little a thing strikes so close to your heart, save that you are yet carnal, and give more heed to please men than you should? And because you fear to be despised, you will not gladly be reproved for your offenses, and you therefore search studiously and busily how you may be excused. But consider yourself well closely, and you will see that the world and a vain love to please men still lives in you. When you refuse to be rebuked and punished for your defects, it appears evident that you are not truly humble, and that you are not yet dead to the world or the world yet truly crucified to you.

But hear My word and you will not need to care for the words of ten thousand men. Lo, if all things that could be most maliciously and untruly invented were said against you, what hurt would they bring, if you suffered them to pass and go away? Truly, no more hurt than a straw under your foot, and they could not take one hair from your head.

But he who does not have a manly heart within himself and does not hold God before the eye of his soul is soon moved by a sharp word, whereas he who trusts in Me and will not stand as his own judge will be free from all fear of man, for I am the Judge who knows all secrets. I know how everything is done and I also know both him who does the wrong and him to whom it is done. This is done by Me; with My permission it comes about. So that the thoughts of men's hearts may be known when the time comes, I shall judge both the innocent and the guilty, but first, through My just examination, I will test them both. The testimony of man often deceives, but My judgment is true and cannot be subverted. And though sometimes it is hidden and known but to few, it is always true and does not err, nor can it err, though in the sight of some unwise person it seems to.

Therefore, in every doubt it behooves you to come to Me and not to lean much on your own reason, but to be content with anything I may send you. A righteous man is never troubled with anything I may permit to happen to him, insomuch as, though a thing were spoken untruly against him, he would not much care, nor would he much rejoice if he were sometimes excused for good reason. He thinks always that I am He who searches a man's heart, and that I do not judge according to the outward appearance, for, often, what in man's sight seems most worthy to be praised will be found in My sight worthy to be blamed.

O Lord God, most just Judge, strong and patient, who knows the frailty and the malice of man, be my strength and comfort in all necessities, for my own conscience, Lord, is not sufficient for me, and You know in me what I do not know. Therefore, I ought always to humble myself under every reproof, and patiently to suffer all things in charity, according to Your pleasure. Forgive me, Lord, as often as I have not done so, and give me the grace of greater patience in time to come. Your mercy is a more profitable and certain way for me to obtain pardon and forgiveness of my sins than a trust in my own works through the defense of my darkened conscience. And though I do not fear my own conscience, I cannot for that reason justify myself, for, if Your mercy is taken away, no man can be justified or appear just in Your sight.

47. How All Grievous Things in This Life Are Gladly to be Suffered for Winning the Life That Is to Come

My son, says our Lord, do not be broken by impatience with the labor you have taken for My sake, or suffer tribulation to cast you into despair, or in any way into unreasonable depression and anguish; be comforted and strengthened in every happening by My promises and commands. I am able and powerful to reward you and My other servants abundantly, more than you can think or desire. You will not labor long here, grieved with despondency. Await My promises a while, and you will at last see an end of all your troubles. An hour will come when all your labors and troubles will cease—and truly, that hour is at hand, for all that passes away with time is short.

Continue, therefore, as you are doing. Labor busily and faithfully in My vineyard, and I will shortly be your reward. Write, read, sing, mourn, be quiet and pray, and suffer adversity gladly, for the kingdom of heaven is worth more than all these things, and is much greater than they. Peace that is known to Me will come one day, and that will not be a day of this life, but a day everlasting with infinite clarity, steadfast peace, and secure rest without end. And then you will not say: Who is to deliver me from the body of this death; nor will you need to cry: Woe to me that my coming to the kingdom of heaven is thus prolonged, for death will then be destroyed, and health of body and soul will be without end, insomuch that there will be no manner of restlessness, but blessed joy and sweetest and most fair company.

Oh, if you saw the everlasting crowns of My saints in heaven, if you saw in how great joy and glory they are who sometimes seemed to be despised in the world, you would soon humble yourself low to the ground, and you would rather to be subject to all men than to have authority over any one person. You would not desire to have happiness and pleasure in this world, but rather to bear with tribulation and pain, and you would account it a great gain to be considered as nothing among the people. Oh, if these things tasted sweet to you and deeply pierced your heart, you would not dare once to complain of any manner of trouble that should befall you. Are not all painful things and most grievous labors gladly to be endured for joy everlasting? Yes, truly. It is no little thing to win or lose the kingdom of heaven.

Lift up your face, therefore, to heaven, and behold how I and all My saints there with Me had great struggle and conflict in this world, yet now they rejoice with Me and are comforted in Me and are sure to abide in Me and to dwell with Me in the kingdom of My Father without end.

48. *Of the Day of Eternity, and of the Miseries of This Life*

O blessed mansion of the heavenly city, O most clear day of eternity, which the night cannot darken, but which the high Truth that is God, illumines and makes clear, always joyful, always secure, and never changing its state into the opposite! Would to God that that day might now appear and shine upon us and that these temporal things were at an end. That blessed day shines on the saints in heaven with everlasting brightness and clarity; to us pilgrims on earth, it shines only afar off, as in a mirror or glass. The heavenly citizens know well how joyful that day is, but we exiles, the children of Eve, weep and bewail the bitterness and weariness of this day, that is, of this present life, short and evil, full of sorrows and anguish, where man is often defiled by sin, encumbered by passion, disquieted by dread, bound by cares, bruised by vanities, blinded by errors, overburdened with labors, vexed by temptations, overcome by the delights and pleasures of the world, and sometimes grievously tormented by poverty and need.

Oh, when will the end of all these miseries come, and when will I be delivered from the bondage of sin? When will I, Lord, have my mind only on You, and be made fully glad and merry in You? When will I be free from hindrance and in perfect liberty, without grief of body or of soul? When will I have steady peace without trouble, peace within and without, and on every side steadfast and sure? O Lord Jesus, when will I stand and behold You, and have full sight and contemplation of Your glory? When will You be to me all in all? When will I be with You in Your kingdom, which You have ordained for Your elect from the beginning?

I am left here poor and as an alien in the land of my enemies, where there are daily battles and great misfortune. Comfort my exile, assuage my sorrow, for all my desire cries to You. Whatever the world offers me here for my solace is to me a grievous burden. I desire to have inward fruitful growth in You, but I cannot attain to it. I desire to cleave fast to heavenly things, but temporal things and unmortified passions pull me always downward. In mind, I would be above all temporal things; but whether I would or not, I am compelled through my own fault to be subject unto my own flesh.

Thus, most wretched man, I fight within myself and become burdensome to myself, while my spirit desires to soar and my flesh is earthbound. Oh, what do I suffer inwardly when in my mind I behold heavenly things and a great multitude of carnal thoughts soon enters my soul! Therefore, Lord, be not far away from me, and depart not in Your wrath from me, Your servant. Send me the light of Your grace and break down in me all carnal thoughts; send forth the darts of Your love, and by them break up all stratagems of the enemy; gather my mind and the powers of my soul together in You; make me forget all worldly things and grant me to cast away and wholly to despise all fantasies of sin. Help me, everlasting Truth, so that no worldly vanity may hereafter have power within me. Come also, heavenly Sweetness, and let all bitterness of sin flee far from me.

Pardon me and mercifully forgive me when in my prayer I think of anything but You. I confess as true that in times past I have behaved myself very inconstantly in my prayer, and many times am not where I sit or stand, but where my thoughts lead me. What pleases me best to think upon comes into my mind, and where my thought is accustomed to be, there is what I love. And so, You who are everlasting Truth says openly: Where your treasure is, there is your heart. Wherefore, if I love heaven, I speak gladly of heavenly things and of such things as concern God and pertain most to His honor, and to the glory and worship of His holy Name. If I love the world, I soon rejoice at worldly happiness and soon sorrow at adversity. If I love the flesh, I imagine often what pleases the flesh, and if I love my soul, I delight much to speak and to hear of things that are for my soul's health. And so, whatever I love, I gladly hear and speak of it, and bear the thoughts of it often in my mind.

Blessed is the man who, for the Lord's sake, forgets all created things and learns truly to overcome himself, and who with fervor of spirit crucifies his flesh so that with a clean and pure conscience he may offer his prayers to You, and be worthy to have the company of the blessed angels, excluding and fully setting aside all earthly things.

49. Of the Desire of Everlasting Life, and of the Great Reward That Is Promised to Them Who Strongly Fight against Sin

My son, when you feel that a desire of everlasting bliss is given to you and that you desire to leave the tabernacle of your mortal body, so that you might clearly, without shadow, behold my clarity, then open your heart, and with all the desire of your soul receive that holy inspiration. And give greatest thanks to the high goodness of God that works so worthily for you, so graciously visits you, so fervently stirs you, and so mightily bears you up in order that you do not fall down to earthly pleasures by your own weight. Do not think that that desire comes of yourself or from your own doing, but, rather, that it comes from the gift of grace, and from the loving regard God has for you, that you should profit thereby in humility and virtue, and that you should prepare yourself to be ready at another time for battles to come, and the more surely cleave to God with all the desire and affection of your heart, and study with all your power how you may most purely and most devoutly serve Him. Take heed of this common proverb: The fire often burns, but the flame does not ascend without some smoke. So, in like manner, the desire of some men ascends to heavenly things, yet they are not all free from the smoke of carnal affections. Therefore, they do not always seek what they ask with such desire from God, purely for the honor and love of God. Such, frequently, is your desire, which you show to be so importunate, for **that** desire is not clean and perfect which is mixed with your own advantage. Ask, therefore, not what is agreeable and profitable to you, but what is acceptable and honorable to Me. If you do well and judge aright, you will prefer My commands and My will before all desires and before all things that you can desire besides Me.

I know your desire well. You would now be in the liberty of the glory of the sons of God; the everlasting house and the heavenly country, full of joy and glory, delight you much, but that hour does not yet come. There is still another time to come—a time of labor and of trial. You desire to be filled with the high goodness of heaven, but you cannot come to it now. I am the full reward of man. Await Me until I come, and you will have Me as your reward.

You are yet to be tried here upon earth and more thoroughly tested in many things. Some comfort will be given you, but the fullness of comfort will not yet be granted. Therefore, be comforted in Me, and be strong as well in doing as in suffering things contrary to your will. It behooves you to be clothed in My blood and to be changed into a new man, and you must often do what you would not do, and you must forsake and leave undone what you would do. What pleases others will advance well, and what pleases you will go slowly; what other men say will be well heard, and what you say will be set at naught; others will ask and get what they ask; you will ask and be denied; others will be great and have much glory and praise from the people, no word will be spoken of you; this office or that will be committed to others, and you will be judged unprofitable in everything. Because of these and other like things, nature will murmur and grumble. And you will have a great battle within yourself, if you bear them secretly in your heart without complaining and contradiction. Nevertheless, in such things and others like them, My faithful servants are wont to be tested: how they can deny themselves and how they can break their own wills in all things.

There is nothing in which you will so much need to overcome yourself as in learning to be content not to have any price set on you in the world, and in suffering such things as are most contrary to your will, especially when such things are commanded to be done as seem unprofitable in your sight. But, My son, consider well the profit and the fruit of these labors, their speedy end and great reward, and then you will feel no grief or pain in all your labors, but the most sweet comfort of the Holy Spirit, because of your good will. For that little will which you forsake here, you will always have your will in heaven where you will have all that you desire. There you will have full possession of all good, without fear to lose it; there you will be ever one with My will, and will desire no strange or singular things; there, no man will resist you, no man complain of you, no man hinder, and none withstand you, but all things that you can desire will there be present, and will fill all the powers of your soul to the full. There I shall give glory for reproof and a cloak of praise for your desolation, and a seat in heaven forever for the lowest place here. There the fruit of obedience will appear, the labor of penance will rejoice, and humble submission will be crowned gloriously.

Bow yourself now, therefore, humbly under man's hand. Regard but little who says this or who commands that to be done, but with all your zeal take heed that, whether your superior or your equal or anyone lower than yourself ask anything of you, or would have you do anything, you always take it for the best, and seek to fulfill it with a glad will. Let this man seek this thing and another man that, and let this man rejoice in this thing and another in that thing, whatever it be, and let them be praised a thousand times, but rejoice yourself neither in this thing nor in that, but only in the contempt and despising that comes to you and in My will to be fulfilled, and that I may always be praised and honored, in you and by you, whether it be by life or death.

50. *How a Man Who Is Desolate Ought to Offer Himself to God*

Lord, holy Father, be You blessed, now and forever. As You will, so it is done, and what You do is always good. Let me, Your poorest and most unworthy servant, rejoice in You and not in myself or in anything else besides You. You, O Lord, are my gladness, You are my hope, my crown, my joy, and all my honor. What does Your servant have, save what he has from You, and that without worthiness? All things You have given and made are Yours.

I am poor and have been in trouble and in pain ever since my youth, and my soul has been in great desolation with great weeping and tears and sometimes it has been troubled within itself through the many passions that come from the world and the flesh. Wherefore, Lord, I desire that I may have from You the joy of inward peace and the repose of Your chosen children whom You feed and nourish in the light of heavenly comfort. Without Your help I cannot attain to it. If You, Lord, give peace or inward joy, my soul will soon be full of heavenly melody, and devout and fervent in Your praise. But if You withdraw Yourself from me, as You have sometimes done, then Your servant cannot run the way of Your commandments as he first did, but he is compelled to bow his knee and to strike his breast, for things are not with him now as they were before, when the lantern of Your spiritual presence shone upon his head and he was defended from all perils and dangers under the shadow of Your mercy.

O just Father, ever to be praised, the time is come in which You have ordained that Your servant should be tested. And it is rightly ordained that I should now suffer something for You. The hour is now come that You have known from the beginning, that your servant should outwardly for a time be set at naught and inwardly live to You, and that he should be despised as little in the sight of the world, and should be broken with passion and sickness, so that he might afterwards rise with You into a new light and be illuminated and made glorious in the kingdom of heaven.

O holy Father, You have ordained it to be so, and it is done as You have commanded. This is Your grace to Your friends, to suffer and to be troubled in this world for Your love, how often soever it be and from person soever it come, and in what manner soever You permit it to fall upon me. Nothing is done upon earth without Your guidance and providence, or without cause. Oh, it is good for me, Lord, that You have humbled me, that I may thereby learn to know Your just judgments and to put from myself all manner of presumption and pride of heart. And it is truly profitable to me that confusion has covered my face, so that I may learn by it to seek help and assistance from You rather than from man. I have thereby learned to fear Your secret and terrible judgment that scourges the just man together with the sinner, but not without equity and justice.

I give thanks that You have not spared my sin, but have punished me with the scourges of love and have sent me sorrows and anguish within and without, so that there is no creature under heaven that can comfort me, save You, Lord God, heavenly Physician of man's soul, who strike and heal and bring a man close to bodily death and afterwards restore him to health again, so that he may thereby learn to know the littleness of his own power and to trust more fully in You.

Your discipline has fallen upon me and Your rod of correction has taught me. Under that rod I wholly submit myself; strike my back and my bones and make me bow my crooked will to Your will; make me a meek and humble disciple, as You have sometimes done with me, that I may walk according to Your will. To You I commit myself and all that is mine, to be corrected, for it is better to be corrected by You here than in time to come. You know all things and nothing in man's conscience is hidden from You. You know things to come before they happen, and it is not necessary for any man to teach You or warn You of anything that is done upon earth. You know what is helpful for me, and how much tribulation helps to remove from me the rust of sin. Do with me according to Your pleasure, and do not disdain my sinful life, known so well by none as by You.

Grant me, O Lord, to know what is necessary to be known, to love what is to be loved, to praise what pleases You highly and to esteem what appears precious in Your sight and to refuse what is vile before You. Permit me not to judge according to my outward intelligence, and not to give sentence according to the judgment of unwise men, but in true judgment to discern things visible and invisible and above all always to search and follow Your will and pleasure. The outward intelligence of men is often deceived in their judgments and in like manner the lovers of the world are deceived through loving only visible things. How is a man better just because he is thought to be better? Truly, in no way, for one deceitful man deceives another, one vain man deceives another, and a blind and feeble creature deceives another when he exalts him and confounds rather than praises him. Why? Whatever a man be worth in the sight of God, says the humble St. Francis, so much is he and no more, no matter how holy and how virtuous he is taken to be in the sight of the people.

51. *That It Is Good for a Man to Give Himself to Humble Bodily Labors, When He Does Not Feel Himself Disposed to High Works of Devotion*

My son, you cannot always stand in the high fervent desire of virtue or in the highest degree of contemplation, but you must, of necessity, because of the corruption of original sin, sometimes descend to lower things, and against your will and with great weariness bear the burden of this corruptible body. For as long as you bear this body of death, you must feel some tediousness and grief of heart, and you will often bewail and mourn the burden of your fleshly feelings and the contradiction of your body to your soul. For you cannot, because of the corruption of your body, persevere in spiritual studies and in heavenly contemplation as you would.

Then it is good for you to flee to humble, bodily labor, and to exercise yourself in good outward works and, in a steady outward trust, to await My coming and My new heavenly visitation and to bear patiently the exile and the dryness of your heart, until you again shall be visited by Me and delivered by Me from all tediousness and disquiet of mind. When I come, I shall make you forget all your former labors and have inward rest and quiet of soul. I shall also lay open before you the flourishing meadow of Holy Scripture, and with great gladness of heart in a new, blessed feeling you will know the truest understanding of it. Then you will run quickly the way of My commandments and will say in great spiritual joy: The sufferings of this world are not worthy of themselves to bring us to the joy that will be shown us in the bliss of heaven. To this bliss, O Lord Jesus, bring us.

52. *That a Man Should Not Think Himself Worthy to Have Comfort, but Rather, to Have Sorrow and Pain, and of the Profit of Contrition*

Lord, I am not worthy to have Your consolation or any spiritual visitation, and therefore You act justly toward me when You leave me needy and desolate. Though I might weep the water of tears like to the sea, I would not be worthy to have Your solace. I am worthy to have nothing but sorrow and pain, for I have so grievously and so often offended You and in so many things trespassed against You. Therefore, I may say well and confess as true that I am not worthy to have Your least consolation. But You, Lord, kind and merciful, who will not have Your work perish, and in order to show the greatness of Your mercy, You deign sometimes to comfort me, Your servant, above all my merit or desert, more than I can think or know.

Your consolations are not like men's fables, for they are in themselves certain and true. But what have I done, Lord, that You deign to give me any heavenly consolation? I do not know that I have done anything as well as I should, though I do know that I have always been prone and ready to sin and slow to amend. This is true. I cannot deny it. If I should deny it, You would stand against me and no man would defend me. What have I deserved, then, but hell and everlasting fire? I confess in truth that I am worthy in this world of all shame and contempt, and that it is not fitting for me to be a familiar of devout people. And though it be grievous to me to say it, I will confess the truth as it is, and openly reproach myself for my defects, that I may the sooner obtain Your mercy and forgiveness. But what may I then say, Lord, who am thus guilty and full of confusion? Truly, I have no mouth or tongue to speak anything but this word: I have sinned, Lord, I have sinned; have mercy on me. Forgive me, and overlook my trespass. Permit me to weep a little and to bewail my sins before I pass hence to the land of darkness, covered with the shadow of death.

And what do You ask most, O Lord, of such a wretched sinner save that he be contrite and humble himself for his sins? For in true contrition and humility of heart is found the very hope of forgiveness of sin, and the troubled conscience is thereby cleared, and grace before lost is again recovered. Man is also thereby defended from the wrath to come, and Almighty God and the penitent soul meet in the holy embrace of heavenly love.

Humble contrition of heart is to You, O Lord, a most acceptable sacrifice, which savors more sweetly in Your sight than burning incense. It is the precious ointment shed upon Your blessed feet, for You never despise a humble and a contrite heart. This contrition is the place of refuge from the fear and wrath of the enemy, and whatever has been done amiss or defiled by sin in any way, is by contrition washed and cleansed.

53. *That Grace Will Not Be Mixed with Love of Worldly Things*

My son, grace is a precious thing, and will not be mixed with any personal love or with any worldly comfort. It behooves you to cast aside all impediments to grace if you would have the gracious gift of it. Choose, therefore, a secret place and love to be alone, and keep yourself from hearing vain tales and fables. Offer to God devout prayers and ask earnestly that you may have a contrite heart and a pure conscience. Think all the world as nothing and prefer My service before all things, for you cannot have your mind fixed on Me and at the same time delight in transitory pleasure. It behooves you, therefore, to withdraw from your dearest friends and from all your acquaintances, and to seclude your mind wholly from the inordinate desire of worldly comfort as much as you can. St. Peter prayed that all Christian people might consider themselves as strangers and as pilgrims upon earth, for then they would set but little price on the comforts of earth.

Oh, how sure a trust it will be to a man, when he departs out of this world, to feel inwardly in his soul that no earthly love or the affection of any passing or transitory thing has domination in him; but a weak person, newly turned toward God, cannot so easily have his heart severed from earthly affections, and the worldly-minded man does not know the freedom of a man who is inwardly turned to God. Therefore, if a man will be perfectly spiritual, he must renounce kinsfolk as well as strangers, and before all else he must particularly beware of himself, for, if he overcome himself perfectly, he will the sooner overcome all other enemies. The most noble and most perfect victory is for a man to have victory over himself. He, therefore, who holds himself so much in submission that sensuality obeys his reason, and his reason in all things obeys Me, he is the true conqueror of himself and the lord of the world.

But if you desire to come to that state, you must begin manfully, and set your axe to the root of the tree, and fully cut away in you all the inordinate inclination that you have toward yourself or any personal or material thing. On this vice, namely, that a man loves himself inordinately, rests very nearly everything that ought be destroyed in man from the roots. And if this be truly overcome, there will soon follow great tranquility and peace of conscience. But insomuch as there are but few who labor to die to themselves and to overcome themselves perfectly, they remain in their fleshly feelings and worldly comforts and can in no manner rise up in spirit above themselves. It behooves him who would be free in heart and contemplate Me to mortify all evil inclinations that he has toward himself and the world and not to be bound to any creature by inordinate or personal love.

54. *Of the Difference between Nature and Grace*

My son, take good heed of the motions of nature and grace, for they are very subtle and very contrary one to the other, and they can be recognized apart with difficulty, unless it be by a spiritual man who is inwardly illuminated in his soul by grace. Every man desires some goodness and pretends to some goodness in all his words and deeds, and so, under the pretense of goodness, many are deceived.

Nature is wily and full of deceit, and draws to herself many whom she often traps and deceives; she always looks to her own gain as the end and purpose of her work. But grace walks simply, without deceit, and turns aside from all evil and pretends no guile; but she does all things purely for God, in whom she finally rests.

Nature will not easily die, or easily be suppressed and overcome. Neither will she easily be under guidance, nor kept in subjection; but grace studies how to be mortified to the world and to the flesh. Grace resists sensuality, seeks to be subject, desires to be subdued, will not use its own liberty. Grace loves to be kept under holy discipline, and does not desire to have domination over any creature, but always to live and stand under the fear of God, and is always ready for His love to bow herself humbly under every creature.

Nature labors for her own profit and advantage and considers much what gain can come from others; grace does not consider what is profitable to herself, but what is profitable to many. Nature gladly accepts honor and reverence; grace refers all honor and reverence to God. Nature fears rebukes and to be despised; grace rejoices to endure them in the name of God and to receive them as special gifts of God when they come. Nature loves idleness and bodily rest; grace cannot resist doing good and therefore joyfully seeks profitable labor.

Nature desires pleasant and unusual things; grace takes joy in humble and simple things, does not despise hard things, and does not refuse to be clad in poor clothing and simple garment.

Nature gladly beholds things of this world; she rejoices at worldly gain, is depressed by worldly loss, and is soon shaken by a sharp word. But grace beholds everlasting things, does not trust in temporal things, and is not troubled by the loss of them, or grieved by intemperate words, for grace has put her treasure in God and in spiritual things that do not perish. Nature is greedy, and takes more gladly than she gives; she loves much to have property and private possessions. But grace is sympathetic and generous to the poor, flees her own gain, is content with little, and judges that it is better to give than to receive.

Nature inclines to the love of creatures, to the love of the flesh, to vanity and gadding about, and to behold novelties in the world. But grace draws a man to love of God and of virtue, renounces all created things, flees the world, hates the desires of the flesh, restrains liberty and wandering about, and avoids as much as she can to be seen consorting with people. Nature receives gladly any outward consolation by which she may be sensibly delighted; grace seeks only to be comforted in God, and to delight in His goodness above all things.

Nature does everything for her own gain and personal profit. She does nothing generously, but always hopes to get equal or better advantage or praise or favor from the people, and desires much that her deeds and works be greatly considered and praised. But grace seeks no temporal thing and no other reward for her employment, save God alone. Grace will have no more of temporal goods than is necessary for the winning of everlasting goods, and does not care for the vain praise of the world.

Nature rejoices greatly in many friends and kinsfolk, and is much puffed by a noble place of birth and noble blood and kindred. Nature has great joy with distinguished men, she flatters rich men, and is happy with those she thinks, like itself, in high worldly position. But grace makes a man love his enemies; she has no pride in worldly friends, does not regard the nobility of kindred or her paternal home, unless virtue dwells there. Grace favors the poor more than the rich; she sympathizes more with an innocent man than with a powerful man; she always rejoices in truth rather than falsehood, and strengthens good men more and more to profit and grow in virtue and goodness, and daily to seek higher gifts of grace so that they may, through good virtuous works, be made like to the Son of God. Nature promptly complains for the lack of a very little thing she would have, or because of a small worldly grief; grace gladly bears all penury and want in the world. Nature draws all things, as much as she can, to herself and to her own profit; she argues for herself and strives and fights for herself. But grace renders all to God, from whom all originally flows and springs. Grace ascribes no goodness to herself and does not presume of herself; she does not strive and prefer her own opinions before others, but in every opinion submits herself humbly to the eternal wisdom and judgment of God.

Nature desires to know and hear new secret things; she yearns that her works be openly displayed, and to have experience of many things in the world by her outward senses; she desires also to be known and to do great things in the world, so that admiration and praise may follow. But grace does not care for any new or curious things, whatever they be, for she knows well that all such vanities arise from the corruption of sin and that nothing new can long endure upon earth. Grace instructs us to control the outward senses, and to avoid all vain pleasure and external show, and humbly keeps secret things that would greatly be marveled at and praised in the world. And in all things and in all knowledge, grace seeks some spiritual profit for herself, and praise and honor for Almighty God. Grace does not desire that her own good deeds or inward devotion be known to others, but desires most that our Lord should be blessed in all His works, who gives all things freely through His high, excellent charity.

This grace is a light from heaven, and a spiritual gift of God. It is the proper mark and token of the elect, and a presage of everlasting life. It lifts a man from the love of earthly things to the love of heavenly things, and makes a worldly man heavenly. The more nature is suppressed and overcome, the more grace is given, and through new, gracious visitations the soul is daily shaped anew, and formed more and more to the image of God.

55. *Of the Corruption of Nature and the Worthiness of Grace*

O Lord God, who have made me to Your own image and likeness, give me this grace You have shown to be so great and so necessary to the health of my soul, so that I may overcome this wretched nature that draws me always to sin and toward the loss of my own soul. I feel in my flesh the law of sin strongly fighting against the law of spirit and leading me like a servant and slave to obey sensuality in many things; I cannot resist the passions of sensuality unless Your grace assists me.

I have, therefore, great need of Your grace, and of Your grace in great abundance, if I would overcome this wretched nature, which from my youth has always been ready and prone to sin. After nature was defiled and vitiated by the sin of the first man, Adam, the penalty descended to all his posterity so that man's nature, which was good and just at creation, is now captured for sin and corruption, insomuch that his purely natural inclinations always attract him to evil. And so, the small strength and inclination to good that still remain in man's nature are like a little spark of fire that is hidden and covered with ashes. That is to say, man's natural reason, which is all surrounded and covered by the darkness of ignorance, nevertheless still has power to judge between good and evil, and to estimate the distance and the diversity between true and false. However, through weakness, it is not able of itself to live up to what is approved, and has not, since the first sin of Adam, the full light of truth or the sweetness of affection toward God it first had.

And so it comes about, most merciful Lord, that inwardly in the thoughts of my soul I delight in Your laws and in Your teachings, knowing that they are good, just, and holy, and that all sin is evil and to be fled and avoided. Yet outwardly, that is to say, in my human sensibility, I serve the law of sin when I bow down to sensuality rather than to reason. And from this it follows that I will to do good, but I cannot, through my weakness, perform the good without Your grace. And sometimes I determine to do many good deeds, but because the grace that would help me is lacking, I fall back and fail in my performance. I know the way to perfection and I see clearly what I should do, but I am so oppressed by the heavy burden of this corrupt body of sin that I lie still and do not rise to perfection. O Lord, how necessary to me, therefore, is Your grace, to begin well, to continue well and to end well, for without You I can do nothing good.

O heavenly grace, without which our merits are worth nothing and all the gifts of nature to be reckoned as as nothing, without which skill or riches are to be esteemed as nothing, and without which beauty, strength, intelligence, and eloquence avail nothing, come quickly and help me! The gifts of nature are common to good men and to bad men, but grace and love are the gifts of the elect and chosen people, by which they are marked and made able and worthy of attaining the kingdom of heaven. This grace is of such worthiness that neither the gift of prophecy, nor the working of miracles, nor the gift of wisdom and knowledge is worth anything without it; even faith, hope or other virtues are not acceptable to You without grace and charity.

O blessed grace that makes the poor in spirit rich in virtue, and makes him who is rich in worldly goods to be humble and submissive in heart, come and descend into my soul and fill me with your spiritual comfort, so that my soul may not fail or faint because of its own weariness and dryness! I beseech You, Lord, that I may find grace in Your sight, for Your grace will be sufficient to me, even though I lack what nature desires. Though I am worried and vexed by troubles on every side, I will not need to fear while Your grace is with me. It is my strength, my comfort, my counsel and my help. It is stronger than all my enemies, and wiser than all the wisest of this world. Your grace is the mistress of truth, the teacher of discipline, the light of the heart. It is the comfort of trouble, the banisher of desolation, the avoider of dread, the nourisher of devotion, and the bearer of sweet tears and devout weeping. Without grace, then, what am I but a dry stick to be cast away? Grant, therefore, that Your grace may go before me and follow me, and make me ever busy and diligent in good works unto my death. So may it be.

56. *That We Ought to Forsake Ourselves and Follow Christ by Bearing His Cross*

My son, as much as you can abandon yourself and your own will, so much will you enter into Me. And as to desire nothing outwardly brings peace to a man's soul, so a man, by an inward forsaking of himself, joins himself to God. It is My will, therefore, that you learn to have a perfect abandonment of yourself and a full resignation of yourself into My hands, without contradicting or complaining, and follow Me, for I am the Way, I am the Truth, and I am the Life. Without a way, no man can go; without the truth, no man can know; and without life no man can live. I am the Way by which you ought to go, the Truth you ought to believe, and the Life you ought to hope to have. I am the Way that cannot be made foul, the Truth that cannot be deceived, and the Life that will never have an end. I am the Way most straight, the Truth most perfect and the Life most certain, a blessed Life and an uncreated Life that created all things. If you dwell and abide in My way, you will know the truth, and the truth will deliver you and you will come to everlasting life.

If you would come to that life, keep My commandments; if you would know the truth, believe My teaching; if you would be perfect, sell all that you have. If you would be My disciple, forsake yourself; if you would possess the blessed life, despise this present life; if you would be exalted in heaven, humble yourself here on earth; and if you would reign with Me, bear the Cross with Me, for, truly, only the servants of the Cross will find the life of blessedness and of everlasting light.

O Lord Jesus, inasmuch as Your way is narrow and straight and is, as well, much despised by the world, give me grace gladly to bear the contempt of the world. There is no servant greater than his lord, and no disciple who is above his master. Let Your servant, therefore, be exercised in Your ways, for in them is the health and the very perfection of life. Whatever I read or hear, beside that way, does not refresh me or fully delight me.

My son, inasmuch as you know these things and have read them all, you will be blessed if you fulfill them. He who has My commandments and keeps them is the one who loves Me, and I will love him and show Myself to him, and make him sit with Me in the kingdom of My Father. Lord, be it done to me as You have said and promised. I have taken the Cross of penance from Your hands and I will bear it unto death as You have directed me to do. The life of every good man is the Cross, and it is also the way and guide to paradise. And now that it has begun, it is not lawful for me to turn my back upon it or proper for me to abandon it.

Have done, therefore, my well-beloved brethren; let us go forth together. Jesus will be with us; for Jesus we have taken this Cross, for Jesus let us persevere, and He who is our Guide and Leader will be our help. Lo, our King who fights for us will go before us. Let us follow Him boldly, let us fear no perils, but be ready to die for Him manfully in battle, so that we place no blot upon our glory, or diminish our reward by fleeing like cowards away from the Cross.

57. That a Man Should Not Be Too Much Cast into Discouragement, though He Happen to Fall into Some Defects

My son, patience and humility in adversity please Me more than much consolation and devotion in prosperity. Why are you so much oppressed by a little word said or something done against you? If it had been more you would not have been so moved by it. But now, let it pass; it is not the first and will not be the last, if you live long. You are manful enough, as long as no adversity befalls you and you can well give counsel, and well comfort and strengthen others by your words. But when adversity knocks at your own door, you soon fail, both in counsel and in strength. Behold well, therefore, your great frailty, of which you have daily experience in little temptations. Nevertheless, it is for your spiritual help that such things and others like them are allowed to happen to you.

Resolve in your heart to do the best that lies in you, and then, when any such tribulation happens to fall to your lot, although it grieve you, do not let it entirely overthrow you, and do not let it long remain with you; at least, bear it patiently, if you cannot bear it gladly. Moreover, even though you loathe to hear such things and though you feel great indignation over them in your heart, hold yourself low in your own sight and permit no inordinate word to pass your lips by which any other person might be hurt. Then all such indignation will soon be calmed and appeased in you, and what before caused you great desolation will soon become sweet and pleasant in your sight, for I still live, says our Lord, ready to help and to comfort you, more than ever before, if you will fully trust in Me, and call upon Me for help.

Be quiet in heart, prepare yourself for yet more suffering, for all is not lost, even though you feel yourself often troubled and grievously tempted. Remember, you are a man and not God; a man of flesh, and no angel. How can you always stand in one state of virtue, when that was not given to the angels in heaven or to the first man in paradise, who did not long stand firm. I am He who raises those who are sorrowful to help and comfort, and lifts up those who know their own unsteadiness to be grounded firm in the sight of my Godhead forever.

Lord, blessed be Your holy word. It is sweeter to my mouth than honeycomb. What would I do in all my troubles and oppression if You did not sometimes comfort me with Your sweet and wholesome words? Therefore, it does not matter what trouble or adversity I suffer here for You, so that I may in the end come to the port of everlasting salvation. Give me a good end and a blessed passage out of this world. Have regard for me, my Lord and my God, and direct me by a straight and ready way into Your kingdom.

58. *That a Man Shall Not Search the Judgments of God*

My son, beware not to dispute of high matters and of the secret judgments of God: why this man is so abandoned and forsaken by God, and why this man is given so great grace; why, also, one man is so much troubled, and another is so greatly advanced. These things surpass all man's knowledge and no man's reason or inquisition can suffice to search God's judgments. Therefore, when the spiritual enemy stirs you to such things or if any inquisitive man ask you such questions, answer with the prophet David, and say: Lord, You are just and Your judgments are true, and are justified in themselves. My judgments are to be feared and not to be discussed by man's reason, for they are incomprehensible to that reason.

Beware also not to search or reason about the merits of the saints: which of them was holier than others or which of them is higher in heaven. Such questions, that is, when one labors to prefer this saint, or another that saint, often foster great strife and unprofitable reasonings, and proceed from vain pride and glory from which envy and dissension spring. Truly, a desire to know such things displeases the saints rather than pleases them. For, says our Lord, I am not God of dissension and strife, but of unity and peace, and peace stands rather in true humility than in pride and vainglory. Some men are more moved to love this saint or that saint with greater affection. But truly, such an affection is often rather a human affection than a divine one. Am I not He who has made all the saints? Yes, truly, and above that I have given them grace and glory. I know all their merits; I ran before them with the sweetness of My blessing; I knew My elect and chosen people before the world was

195

made. I have chosen them out of the world; they have not chosen Me. I called them by My grace, I drew them by My mercy, I led them through temptation, I sent them inward comfort, I gave them perseverance, I crowned their patience. I know the first man and the last. I love them all with an inestimable love.

Thus I am to be praised in all My saints, and above all things to be blessed and honored in all and in every one of them whom I have so gloriously magnified and predestined without any preceding merit of their own. Therefore, he who belittles the least of My saints does no honor to the greatest, for I have made both the less and the greater. And he who belittles any of My saints belittles Me and My other saints in the kingdom of heaven. They are all one, fast-bound and knit together in one sure bond of perfect charity. They feel all alike, and they will all alike, and they love all together in unity; and they love Me much more than themselves or their own merits. They are rapt above themselves and drawn from their own love and wholly turned to My love in which they rest in eternal fruition. There is nothing that can turn them away from My love or thrust them down out of their glory, for they are full of eternal truth and burn inwardly in their souls with the fire of everlasting charity that never will be quenched.

Let all those, therefore, who are carnal-minded and can love only their personal joy, cease to search the state of My blessed saints in heaven, for they subtract from and add to the merit of the saints as they think proper, not according to the eternal truth of God. Many people are in great ignorance, but most especially those who have so little light of spiritual understanding that they cannot love any person with a pure love. Many people are also moved to love this saint or that one, and as they imagine in earthly things, so they imagine in heavenly things. But there is an incomparable distance between things which imperfect men imagine by their natural reason and those things which men truly illumined by heavenly grace behold with heavenly contemplation.

Beware, therefore, my son, not to treat curiously of such things, for they pass your knowledge, but endeavor, instead, that you may be worthy to be numbered among the least saints who will come to heaven. And if, perhaps, a man might know who were holier and who would be considered greater in the kingdom of heaven, what would that knowledge profit him, unless by it he would himself be the more humble, and rise the more to glorify and praise Your Name? Truly, nothing. Therefore, he is more acceptable to God who ponders the greatness of his sins and the littleness of his virtues, and how far he is from the perfection of the least saint in heaven, than he who argues about the greatness or the littleness of the saints, or the blessedness of their life, forgetting himself. It also is better with devout prayer and with weeping and tears humbly to pray to the saints, and to call to them for help, than vainly to inquire after their perfection.

The saints are very well content with the joy they have, if men but would refrain from such useless arguments. The saints do not glorify themselves because of their merits, or ascribe any goodness to themselves, but they refer everything to Me, because they know well that I, of My infinite goodness and charity, have given all to them. And they are so much filled with love of the Godhead and with surpassing joy that no glory and no felicity is lacking to them. And the higher they are in heaven, the more humble they are in themselves, and the closer to Me and the more in love with Me. Therefore, it is written in the Apocalypse that the saints in heaven laid their crowns before God, and fell prostrate on their faces before the humble Lamb, that is, Jesus, and worshipped Him as their Lord God who is and will be living for evermore.

Many who do not know whether they will be worthy to be numbered among the least who will come to heaven argue about who is highest in heaven. It is a great thing to be least in heaven, where all are great, for all who come there will be called the sons of God, and so they indeed will be. The least in heaven will be counted worth a thousand, but a sinner of a hundred years will be set at nothing. When the Apostles asked among themselves who should be the greatest in the kingdom of heaven, they heard this answer from Christ: Unless you are turned from your sin, and become as little children, you cannot enter into the kingdom. He, therefore, who humbles himself like this little child will be the greatest in the kingdom of heaven.

Woe be to them who disdain to humble themselves as little children, for the low gate of heaven will not permit them to enter through it. Woe be to the rich, also, proud men who have their consolation here, for when the good, poor men enter into the kingdom of God, they will stand weeping and wailing without. Rejoice, then, you who are humble and poor in spirit, for yours is the kingdom of heaven, provided you walk and hold your journey steadfastly in the way of truth.

59. *That All Our Hope and Trust Is to be Put in God Alone*

O Lord, what is the trust that I can have in this life, or what is my greatest solace among all things under heaven? Is it not You, my Lord God, whose mercy is without measure? Where have things been well with me without You, and when have things not been well with me if You were present? I would rather be poor with You than rich without You. I would rather be with You a pilgrim in this world, than without You to be in heaven. Where You are is heaven, and where You are not is both death and hell. You are to me all that I desire, and therefore it behooves me to cry to You and heartily to pray to You. I have nothing save You to trust in that can help me in my necessity, for You are my hope, You are my trust, You are my comfort, and You are my most faithful helper in every need.

Man seeks what is his, but You seek my salvation and profit and turn all things to the best for me. If You send temptations and other adversities, You order all to my profit, for You are accustomed to test Your chosen people in a thousand ways. And in such testing You are no less to be glorified and praised than if You had filled your people with heavenly comfort. In You, therefore, Lord, I put my trust, and in You I bear patiently all my adversities, for without You I find nothing but instability and folly. I see well that a multitude of worldly friends is no profit to me, that strong helpers can avail nothing, nor wise counselors give profitable counsel, nor skillful teachers give consolation, nor riches deliver in time of need, nor secret place in any way defend, if You, Lord, do not assist, help, comfort, counsel, instruct, and defend. Everything that seems to be ordained for man's solace in this world is worth nothing if You are absent; nor may all these things bring any man to true happiness, for You, Lord, are the end of all good things. You are the sublimity of life, the profound wisdom of everything that is in heaven and on earth, and so, to trust in You above all things is the greatest comfort to all Your servants. To You, therefore, the Father of mercy, I lift up my eyes; in Thee alone, my Lord, my God, do I put my trust. May my soul bless and hallow You with Your own heavenly blessings, so that it may be Your dwelling place and the seat of Your eternal glory, so that nothing may be found in me at any time that may offend the eye of Your majesty. Behold me, Lord, according to the greatness of Your goodness and Your manifold mercies, and graciously hear my prayer, the prayer of your poorest servant, outlawed and exiled far away in the country of the shadow of death. Defend and keep me among the manifold perils and dangers of this corruptible life, and direct me through Your grace by the ways of peace into the country of everlasting clarity without end.

BOOK IV

Which Treats Especially
of the Sacrament of the Altar

1. With How Great Reverence Christ Is to be Received

Come to Me all you who labor and are heavily burdened, and I will refresh you, says our Lord. And the bread that I will give you will be My Flesh, for the life of the world. Take you and eat: for it is My Body that will be given for you to sacrifice. Do this in remembrance of Me, for whoever eats My Flesh and drinks My Blood, he will dwell in Me, and I in him. These words I have said to you are spirit and life.

O my Lord Jesus Christ, Eternal Truth, these words are Your words, although they were not spoken in one same time or written in one same place. And because they are Your words, I will thankfully and faithfully accept them. They are Your words and you have spoken them, and they are mine also, for You have said them for my salvation. I shall gladly receive them from Your mouth to the end that they may be better sown and planted in my heart. Your words of such great pity, full of sweetness and love, greatly stir me. But, Lord, my sins put me in great fear and my conscience, not pure to receive so great a mystery, holds me sadly aback. The sweetness of Your words stirs me, but the multitude of my offenses weighs most heavily upon me. You command me to come unto You faithfully, if I will have part with You, and to receive the nourishment of immortality, if I yearn to obtain the glory of everlasting life. Lord, You say: Come to me you who labor and are heavily burdened, and I will refresh you. Oh, how sweet and how friendly a word is this in the ear of a sinner, that You, Lord God, will bid me, so poor and needy, to the communion of Your most holy Body. But what am I, Lord, that I dare presume to come to You. Lo, heaven and earth may not comprehend You, and yet You say: Come all of you to Me.

What is the meaning of this humble familiarity and this lovely and friendly invitation? How shall I, who do not know that I have done anything well, dare come to You? How shall I, who have so often offended before Your face, bring You into my house? Angels and archangels honor you and just men fear You, yet You say: Come all of you to Me. Except that You, Lord, said it, who would believe it to be true? Except that You commanded it, who would dare approach?

That just man, Noe, labored a hundred years to make an ark, so that he might be saved with a few of his people. How can I, then, prepare myself in an hour to receive with due reverence You who are Maker and Creator of all the world?

Moses, Your servant and special friend, made the ark of the covenant of undecaying timber, which he covered with most pure gold, and put in it the tables of the Law. How shall I, a corrupt creature, so easily dare to receive You, the Maker of the Law, and Giver of grace and life to all creatures? Wise Solomon, King of Israel, built in the space of seven years a marvelous temple to the praise of Your name, and for eight days sanctified the feast of its dedication. He offered a thousand peace offerings and put the ark of God in the place prepared for it, with great melody of clarions and trumpets. How, then, dare I, who am the poorest of all creatures and scarcely have spent one hour of time or one half-hour of my life well, receive You into my house? O my good

Lord, how much they studied to please You and how little is what I do! How little time do I take, when I prepare myself for Communion! Seldom am I recollected in You and more seldom still am I purified from giving my mind overmuch to worldly things. Certainly, no unprofitable thoughts ought to come into the holy presence of Your Godhead and no creatures ought to have place there, for I am not receiving an angel, but the Lord of angels, into my heart. Moreover, there is a great difference between the ark of God, with its relics, and Your most pure and precious Body, with its virtues, which are more than can be told; between the sacrifice of the Old Law, which was only a figure of the New Law, and the true Host of Your precious Body, that is, the fulfillment of all the old sacrifice. Why, then, am I not more enflamed to come to You? Why do I not prepare myself with greater diligence to receive this Holy and Blessed Sacrament, since the ancient holy fathers, the patriarchs and prophets, kings and princes, with all the people, showed in time past so great affection toward your service? The most devout and blessed ruler, King David, went before the ark of God and honored it with all his strength, always remembering the great benefits given before to the fathers. He made musical instruments of different kinds and composed the Psalms which he ordered to be sung and which he himself sang with great gladness. And often, being filled with the grace of the Holy Spirit, he taught the people of Israel with his harp to glorify and praise God with all their heart, and daily with their mouth to bless Him and preach His goodness. And if so great devotion and remembrance of the glory and praise of God before the ark of the Old Testament was manifest then, how much reverence and devotion ought we now have in the presence of this holy Sacrament and in the reception of the most excellent Body of our Lord, Jesus Christ.

Many run off to different places to visit the relics of the saints, and greatly marvel when they hear of the saints' blessed deeds. They see great buildings of temples and behold how the saints' holy relics are wrapped with silk and covered with gold, and lo, You, my Lord God, the most holy Saint of saints, the Creator of all things and the Lord of angels, are here present to me upon the altar. There often is great curiosity and vanity in the sight of the saints' temples and relics, and little fruit or amendment of life is obtained by them, especially where there is much frivolous assembling and wandering about, without any prior contrition. But You, my Lord God, my Lord Jesus Christ, God and man, You are here wholly present in the Sacrament of the altar, where the fruit of everlasting salvation is plentifully obtained, as often as You are worthily and devoutly received. But if that is to be done fruitfully, there can be no levity, no curiosity or sensuality, but only steadfast faith, devout hope, and pure charity.

O God invisible, Creator of all the world, how marvelously do you deal with us! How sweetly and how graciously do You dispose all things for your chosen people, to whom You offer Yourself to be received in this glorious Sacrament! Certainly, it surpasses all understanding and draws the heart and enkindles the affection of all devout men. True, faithful people who dispose all their lives to amendment often receive through this glorious Sacrament great grace and devotion and great love of virtue.

Oh, the grace of this Sacrament is marvelously and secretly hidden, and only the faithful people of God know it, for infidels and those who live in sin can have no sort of experience of it. In this Sacrament spiritual grace is given, and virtue that was lost is restored, and the beauty that was deformed by sin returns again; and the grace of this Sacrament is sometimes so much that, from the fullness of devotion that comes with it, not only the mind but also stricken bodies recover their former strength.

Truly, it is a cause of great sorrow that we are so slow

and negligent, and that we are stirred no more than we are with affection to receive Christ, for in Him rests all the merit and hope of those who will be saved. He is our salvation and our redemption; He is the Comforter of all who live in this world and the eternal rest of the saints in heaven, and it is a cause of great sorrow that so many little regard this high mystery which rejoices heaven and preserves all the world. Alas for the blindness and hardness of man's heart which takes no greater heed of so noble a gift, but becomes negligent and heedless even in its daily use. If the Blessed Sacrament were administered in one place only and consecrated by one priest in the whole world, with how great desire, do you think, would people run to that place and to that priest, so that they might there behold these heavenly mysteries! Now there are many priests and Christ is offered in many places, so that as Holy Communion is spread the more abroad throughout the world, the grace and love of God to man may the more appear.

Thanks be to You, therefore, my Lord Jesus, that You deign to refresh us poor exiles with Your precious Blood and to stir us up with the words of Your own mouth to receive this holy mystery, saying: Come to Me all you who labor and are heavily burdened, and I will refresh you.

2. *That the Great Goodness of God Is Given to Man in the Blessed Sacrament*

O my Lord Jesus, trusting in Your goodness and mercy, I come to You as a sick man comes to him who will heal him, and as a hungry and thirsty man to the Fountain of life, as a needy man to the King of heaven, as a servant to his Lord, as a creature to his Creator, and as a desolate person to his kind and blessed Comforter.

But how is it that You come to me? Who am I that

You give Yourself to me? How dare I, a sinner, appear before You and how is it that You will deign to come to so sinful a creature? You know Your servant and You see well that he has no goodness of himself for which You should give him this grace. I confess, therefore, my own unworthiness and I acknowledge Your goodness. I praise Your pity and give thanks for Your great charity. Truly, You do all this from Your own goodness and not because of my merit. You do it so that Your goodness may thereby the more appear and Your charity the more largely be shown and Your humility the more highly be commended. Therefore, because this pleases You and You have commanded that it should so be done, Your goodness therein pleases me. Would to God that my iniquity did not resist it.

You are the Saint of all saints and I am the lowest of all sinners. Yet to me, who am not worthy to look upward to You, You bow Yourself down. You come to me, You will be with me, You invite me to Your feast. You will give me this heavenly meat and this angels' food which is clearly none other but Yourself who are the living bread who comes down from heaven and gives life to the world. Behold, Lord, whence all this love proceeds, and how great goodness shines upon us, and how great thanks and praises for it are due to You. Oh, how health-giving and how profitable a counsel it was when You ordained this glorious Sacrament, and how sweet and how joyous a feast it was when You gave Yourself as bread to be eaten. O Lord, how marvelous is Your work, how mighty is Your virtue, and how unutterable is Your truth. By Your word all things were made and all things were done as You commanded.

It is a marvelous thing, worthy of all belief and far above the understanding of man, that You, Lord, who are true God and true man, are wholly contained under a little appearance of bread and wine, and are eaten without being consumed by him who receives You, and that You who are Lord of all things and depend on nothing in this world would dwell in us by this glorious Sacrament. Keep my heart and my body immaculate, so that with a glad and pure conscience I may often celebrate the mysteries which You have ordained most especially to Your honor and perpetual memory, and that I may receive them to my own everlasting salvation.

O my soul, be merry and glad for so noble a gift and so singular a comfort left to you in this vale of misery. As often as you remember this mystery and receive the Body of Christ, so often you work the work of your redemption and are made partaker of all the merits of Christ. Truly, the charity of God is never diminished and the greatness of His mercy is never consumed. Therefore, you ought always with renewal of spirit to prepare yourself for the Blessed Sacrament and to think on this great mystery of Redemption with well-instructed and profound recollection. It should seem to you to be as new and pleasant a joy, whenever you celebrate Mass or hear it, as if Christ the same day were entering the womb of the Virgin and were being made man, or as if he had the same day suffered and died upon the cross for the redemption of mankind.

3. That It Is Very Profitable to Receive Communion Often

I come to You, O Lord, so that things may be well with me through Your gift, and that I may rejoice at the holy feast You have made ready for me through Your great goodness. In You is all that I may or should desire, for You are my salvation and my redemption, my hope, my strength, my honor and glory. Make me, Your servant, today merry and glad in You, for I have lifted my soul to You. Now I desire devoutly and reverently to receive You into my house, so that I may deserve with Zacheus to be blessed by You and to find company among the children of Abraham.

My soul desires to receive Your Body, my heart desires to be made one with You. Come to me, Lord, and it is sufficient, for without You there is no comfort. Without You, I cannot be; without Your visitation, I cannot live. Therefore, it behooves me often to go to You and for my health to receive You, lest, if I were deprived of this heavenly meat, I should perhaps fail in the way. So You Yourself said, most merciful Jesus, as You were preaching to the people and healing them of their sickness: I will not let them return to their houses fasting, lest they fail by the way. Do with me, therefore, in like manner, You who have left Yourself in this glorious Sacrament for the comfort of all faithful people.

You are, in truth, the true nourishment of the soul, and he who worthily receives You will be partaker and heir of eternal glory. It is necessary for me, who so often offends, who soon grows dull and slow, to renew myself by frequent prayers and confessions, and to purify myself and kindle myself to alertness and fervor of spirit, lest perhaps by long abstinence from the Blessed Sacrament I fall away from such a holy purpose. The mind of man and woman is, from youth, proud and prone to evil, and unless this heavenly medicine gives help, they may soon fall from worse to worse. Therefore, Holy Communion draws a man away from evil and strengthens him in goodness.

If I am now often negligent and slothful, even when I have been to Communion, what would I be if I had not received that blessed medicine and not sought that great help? And though I am not every day ready or disposed to receive my Creator, I shall take heed to receive Him at the proper times, so that I may be a partaker of so great a grace. It is one of the greatest consolations to a faithful soul that, as long as he is a pilgrim in this mortal body, he often remembers his Lord God, and receives Him who is his only Beloved above all things. It is a marvelous goodness of the great pity that You have taught us, Lord, Creator and Giver of life to all spirits, that You deign to come to so poor a creature and to refresh his hunger and his need with Your divinity and Your humanity. Oh, happy is that man and blessed is that soul who desires devoutly to receive his Lord God, and in the reception to be filled with spiritual joy! Oh, how great a Lord does he receive! How beloved a Guest does he bring into his house! How joyous a Companion does he admit, how faithful a Friend does he accept, how noble a Spouse does he embrace, who receives You, for You alone are to be beloved before and above all others and all things.

Let heaven and earth and all their adornments be silent in Your presence, for whatever they have worthy of glory or praise they have from the bounty of Your gift, O Lord, yet they cannot be compared to the honor and glory of Your Name, of whose wisdom there is no number or measure.

4. *That Many Advantages Are Given to Those Who Devoutly Receive This Holy Sacrament*

O Lord my God, go before Your servant with the blessing of Your sweetness, so that he may deserve to approach this high Sacrament reverently and devoutly; stir my heart to a full sight of You, and deliver me from the great sloth and idleness in which I have been. Visit me in Your goodness and give me grace inwardly to taste in my soul the sweetness that is hid secretly in the most Blessed Sacrament, as in the most abundant fountain. Illumine my eyes also to see and behold so great a mystery, and strengthen me so that I may always faithfully and unswervingly believe it. It is Your operation, and not the power of man; Your holy institution, and not man's invention. Therefore, no man is sufficient unto himself to grasp and understand these things, for they surpass the subtlety of all angels and heavenly spirits.

What can I, then, most unworthy sinner, earth and ashes, understand and grasp of so high a secret, save that in simplicity of heart, in a good, firm faith, and by Your commandment I come to You with humble hope and reverence, and believe truly that You are here present in this Sacrament, God and man. It is Your will, therefore, that I shall receive You, and knit myself to You in perfect charity. Wherefore, I ask mercy of You and desire You to give me Your special grace, so that I may from now on be fully dissolved into Your love, and never afterwards concern myself with any other comforts. This highest and most worthy Sacrament is the life of soul and body, the medicine of all spiritual sickness. By it all vices are cured, all passions are restrained, all temptations are overcome and diminished; by it grace is sent, virtue is increased, faith is made firm, hope is strengthened, charity is kindled and spread abroad.

By this Sacrament You have given and still frequently give many great gifts to Your beloved servants who devoutly receive You. By it You are the strong Upholder of my soul, the Repairer of all the infirmities of man, and the Giver of all inward consolation and of comfort in tribulation. From the depths of their own dejection You raise Your elect again into strong hope that You will preserve them. You renew them and illuminate them inwardly with new grace, so that they, who before receiving the Blessed Sacrament felt themselves sluggish and without affection, have found themselves after its reception changed into great spiritual fervor. All this You do from Your great goodness toward Your elect people, that they may see and know openly from experience that they have nothing of themselves, but that all the grace and goodness they have they have received from You. Of themselves they are cold, dull, and undevout; but by You they are made fervent, quick in spirit, devout followers of Your will. Who can go humbly to the fountain of sweetness without bringing away with him great plenty of sweetness? Or who can stand by a great fire without feeling its great heat? You, Lord, are the Fountain of all sweetness, the Fire always burning and never failing. Therefore, though I may not draw from the fullness of that fountain or drink from it to the full, I will refresh my thirst, so that I shall not be all dried up. And though I am not all spiritual and all burning in charity as the seraphim and cherubim are, I will endeavor to set myself to devotion and to prepare my heart, so that I may get some little spark of the fire of heavenly love through the humble reception of this life-giving Sacrament.

I beseech You, Lord, benignly and graciously to supply in me whatever is lacking in me, for You deign to call all to You, saying: Come to Me, all you who labor and are heavily burdened, and I will refresh you. I labor in the sweat of my body and I am tormented with the sorrow of my heart; I am charged with sin, burdened with temptation, encompassed about and oppressed by many evil passions. There is none who can help or deliver me or make me safe save You, Lord God, my only Saviour, to whom I commit myself and all that is mine, so that You may keep me and lead me into life everlasting. Accept me and take me to the praise and glory of Your Name, You who have prepared for me Your Body and Blood to be my meat and drink. Grant me, Lord, I beseech You, that the fervor of devotion may daily increase in me, by the frequent reception of Your high mysteries.

5. Of the Worthiness of the Sacrament of the Altar, and of the State of the Priesthood

If you had the purity of angels and the holiness of St. John the Baptist, you would not for that reason be worthy to receive or to touch the Holy Sacrament. It is not granted according to the merits of man that a man should consecrate and touch the Sacrament of Christ and to take for his food the Bread of Angels. It is a great mystery and it is the great dignity of priests to whom is granted what is not granted to the angels. Only priests who are duly ordained in the Church have the power to celebrate Mass and to consecrate the Body of Christ. A priest is the minister of God, using the words of consecration by the commandment and ordinance of God, and God is in the Sacrament the principal Doer and the invisible Worker. To God is subject all that He wills and all obey what He commands. You ought, therefore, more to believe Almighty God in this most excellent Sacrament than your own intelligence or any other visible token or sign, and therefore you are to approach this blessed work with fear and reverence. Take heed diligently, therefore, and behold the Source of this ministry and service that is given to you by the imposition of the hands of the bishop.

You are now made a priest and are consecrated to celebrate Mass. Take heed, therefore, to offer your sacrifice to God in due time faithfully and devoutly and to keep yourself without reproof. You have not made your burden more light, but you are now bound by a stricter bond of discipline and of higher perfection than you were before. A priest ought to be adorned with all virtues and to give others the example of a good life. His conversation should not be in the common way of the world, but with angels in heaven or with perfect men on earth who are most disposed to serve God.

A priest clothed in holy vestments takes the place of Christ, so that he should humbly and meekly pray to our Lord for himself and for all the people. He has before him and behind him the sign of the Cross of Christ, so that he should diligently remember His Passion. He bears the Cross before him, so that he may diligently behold and see the steps of Christ and study fervently to follow them; and behind him he is also signed with the Cross, so that he may gladly and humbly suffer all adversities for the love of God. He bears the Cross before him, so that he should bewail his own sins; and he bears the Cross behind him, so that he may through compassion bewail the sins of others and recognize that he is set as a mediator between God and all the people, and not cease from prayer and holy offerings until he deserves the mercy and grace of Almighty God.

When a priest says Mass he honors God; he makes the angels glad; he edifies the Church; he helps the people who are living, and gives rest to those who are dead, and makes himself a partaker of all good deeds.

6. *Of the Inward Remembrance and Exercise That Man Ought to Have before Receiving the Body of Christ*

Lord, when I think of Your worthiness and of my great vileness I tremble strongly and am confounded within myself. If I do not receive You, I flee from eternal life; if I receive You unworthily, I run into Your wrath. What shall I do then, my good Lord, my Helper, my Protector, my Comforter, and most sure Counselor in all necessities?

Teach me, good Lord, the right way, and appoint for me some ready exercise proper to the reception of this holy mystery, for it is necessary and greatly profitable to me to know how devoutly and reverently I ought to prepare my heart to receive it or to consecrate so great and so goodly a sacrifice as this is.

7. Of the Searching of Our Own Conscience and of the Purpose of Amendment

It behooves you above all things to celebrate, take, and receive this Holy Sacrament with sovereign reverence and profound humility of heart and with full faith and humble intention, to the honor of God. Examine your conscience diligently by true contrition and humble confession, and make that conscience clean to your full extent, so that you may be conscious of nothing that grieves or pricks your conscience or can hinder you from going freely to this Sacrament. Let all your sins in general displease you and have special sighs and sorrowing for your daily excesses and offenses; and, if time will permit it, confess the miseries of all your passions unto God in the secret of your own heart.

Weep and be sorrowful that you are yet so carnal and worldly, so unmortified in your passions, so full of the motions of concupiscence, so incautious and ill-ordered in your outward desires, so often entangled in vain fantasy; so much inclined to outward and worldly things, so negligent in inward things; so ready for frivolous behavior and dissoluteness, so slow to weeping and compunction; so prepared for pleasant things and for what delights the flesh, so slow to penance and fervor of spirit; so eager to hear new things and to see fair things; so loath to humble and abject things; so covetous to have much, so niggardly to give, so glad to hold; so unadvised in speaking, so reluctant to be quiet; so ill-ordered in manners, so importunate in deeds; so greedy for nourishment, so deaf to the word of God; so quick to rest, so slow to labor; so attentive to fables, so sleepy in holy vigils; so hasty toward the end, so unstable to take heed of the way to the end; so negligent in the service of God, so dull and undevout, so dry in Communion; so soon dissipated in outward things, so seldom recollected to inward things; so soon moved to anger and wrath, so easily stirred by the displeasure of others; so ready to judge, so rigorous to reprove; so glad in prosperity, so feeble in adversity; so often purposing many good things, and so seldom bringing them to fruition.

And when you have thus confessed and bewailed all these defects in yourself and others like them, with great sorrow and displeasure at your own frailness, set yourself, then, in a full purpose to amend your life and to advance always from better to better. And then, with full resignation and with a whole-hearted will, offer yourself to the honor of My Name on the altar of My heart as a sacrifice to Me. That is to say, commit faithfully to Me both your body and soul, so that you may be worthy to offer to Me this high Sacrifice, and to receive healthfully the Sacrament of My Holy Body.

There is no oblation more worthy nor satisfaction greater to put sin away than for a man to offer himself purely and wholly to God, with the offering of Christ in Mass and in Holy Communion. If a man do all he can and if he is truly penitent, as often as he comes to Me for grace and forgiveness I am the Lord who says: I will not the death of a sinner, but rather that he be converted and live. I shall no more remember his sins, but they will all be forgiven and pardoned him.

8. Of the Oblation of Christ on the Cross, and of a Full Forsaking of Ourselves

Our Lord Jesus says to His servant: As I offered Myself to God the Father for your sins, hanging all naked with My arms spread wide upon the cross, so that nothing remained in Me, but all went in sacrifice to please My Father and to appease His wrath against mankind, so in the Mass you daily ought to offer yourself freely to God as much as you can, as a pure and holy oblation.

What more do I ask of you than that you should study to resign yourself wholly to Me? I do not regard whatever you give Me besides yourself, for I do not look for your gifts, but for you. For, as it should not be sufficient for you to have all things else besides Me, so it will not please Me unless you give Me yourself, whatever else you give. Offer yourself to Me and give yourself all for God, and your oblation will be acceptable.

Lo, I offered Myself wholly to My Father for you, and I gave my Body and Blood to be your meat, so that I should be wholly yours and you wholly Mine. But if you have trust in yourself and do not freely offer yourself to My will, your oblation is not pleasing and there will not be between us a perfect union. A free offering of yourself into the hands of God must precede all your works if you will obtain grace and true liberty. And so it happens that so few are inwardly illuminated and free, because they cannot wholly forsake themselves. My words are true: Unless a man renounce himself, he cannot be My disciple. Therefore, if you desire to be My disciple, offer yourself fully to Me, with all your affection and love.

9. That We Ought to Offer Ourselves and All That Is Ours to God, and Pray for All People

Lord, all things in heaven and in earth are Yours. I desire to offer myself to You in free and perpetual oblation, so that I may forever be with You. Lord, in simplicity of heart, I offer myself this day to You, to be Your servant in service and sacrifice of perpetual praise. Accept me with the oblation of Your precious Body, which this day I offer You in the presence of Your holy angels, here invisibly present, so that it may be to my salvation and to the salvation of all people. Lord, I offer You all the sins and offenses I have committed before You and Your holy angels, from the day I first offended to this day, that You may deign, through Your great charity, to put away all my sins, and to clean my conscience of all my offenses, and to restore to me again the grace I have lost through sin, and to forgive me all past sins, and receive me mercifully to the blessed kiss of peace and forgiveness.

What, then, can I do but humbly confess and bewail my sins and continually ask Your mercy? Forgive me now, merciful Lord, I beseech You, for all my sins displease me much. I will never commit them again. I am sorry for them and I am ready to do penance and satisfaction to my full power. Forgive me, Lord, forgive me my sins for the sake of Your holy Name. Save my soul, which You have redeemed with Your most precious Blood. I commit myself wholly unto Your mercy; I resign myself into Your hands. Do with me according to Your goodness, not according to my malice and wretchedness.

I offer You all my good deeds, though they are very few and imperfect, to the end that You may amend and sanctify them and make them pleasing and acceptable to Yourself, and to the end that You may bring me, though I am a slow and unprofitable servant, to a blessed and glorious end.

I offer You all the desires of devout persons, the needs of my ancestors, friends, brothers, sisters, and all those who love me, and of all those who, for Your love, have done good to me or to any other, and of those who have desired and asked me to pray or to do sacrifice for them or for their friends, living or dead, so that they may the more feel the help of Your grace and the gift of Your heavenly consolation, Your protection from all perils and Your deliverance from all pain, and so that, delivered from all evils, they may give You high praise and glory in spiritual gladness.

I offer You my prayers and my peace offerings for all

those who have in any way hindered me or burdened me, or who have done me any hurt or grief, and for all those whom I have at any time burdened or troubled or grieved or slandered in word or deed, knowingly or unknowingly, to the end that You may forgive us, all together, our sins and offenses against You and of any one of us against another, and that You, Lord, may take from our hearts all suspicion and indignation, wrath, dissension, and whatever else may hinder charity or diminish the fraternal love each of us ought to have for the other.

Have mercy, Lord, have mercy on all those who ask Your mercy, and give grace to those who need it, and make us stand in such condition that we may be worthy to have Your grace and finally to come to everlasting life.

10. *That Holy Communion Is Not Easily to be Neglected*

It behooves you to run often to the fountain of grace and mercy, to the fountain of all goodness and purity, so that you may be healed from your passions and vices, and be made stronger against all temptations and deceitful wiles of the enemy.

The devil, knowing the great fruit and the high remedy there is in receiving the Blessed Sacrament, drives himself on in every way to keep and withdraw from it all faithful and devout persons as far as he can, and therefore some men experience greater temptations than they had before when they dispose themselves to receive the Blessed Sacrament. As it is written in Job: The wicked spirit comes among the children of God so that he may, by his old malice and wickedness, trouble them or make them overly fearful and confused, in order to diminish their affection or take away their faith, on the chance that he may thereby make them either completely cease from Communion or else approach it with little devotion. You should not pay any attention to his wiles and fantasies, however vile and ugly they may be; all illusions are to be thrown back at his own head, and he is to be so despised that Holy Communion is not neglected in spite of all the assaults and commotions he can stir up.

Sometimes excessive scrupulosity over a sense of devotion or too much doubt about making Confession greatly hinder this holy purpose. Act, therefore, after the counsel of wise men and put away all doubts and scrupulosity, for they hinder the grace of God and wholly destroy the devotion of the mind. It is not good for you to leave this holy work undone because of any little trouble or grief, but go quickly and be confessed, and gladly forgive all who have offended you, and if you have offended any other one humbly ask his forgiveness, and God will mercifully forgive you.

What advantage is it to stay away from Confession long or long to put off Holy Communion? Purify yourself first and quickly cast out your venom and hasten out afterwards to take your Medicine, and you will feel more profit in it than if you stay longer away from it. If you defer it today for this or for that reason, a greater reason may come tomorrow, and so you may long be hindered from your good purpose and afterwards become less disposed to it. Therefore, as soon as you can, free yourself from such slowness and dullness of mind, for there is no profit in long being wretched, long being accompanied by trouble, and, because of such daily obstacles, long to keep yourself aloof from the divine mysteries. It does great hurt and commonly brings with it great sloth and lack of devotion. But alas, for sorrow, some slothful and dissolute persons gladly seek causes to put off Confession, and so the longer defer Holy Communion. And they do this with the intention that they should not be bound to hold themselves in check, in the future, more than they did before.

But alas, how little charity and how meager devotion do they have who so easily neglect so holy a thing; and how happy and how acceptable to God is he who so lives and so guards his conscience in purity that he is every day ready and has good affection to receive Communion, if it were proper for him to do so and he might do it without arousing attention or gossip. He is to be praised for his reverence who sometimes abstains from Holy Communion through humility or for any other lawful reason; but if he abstains through sloth, he ought to bestir himself and do all that is in him, and our Lord will strengthen his desire because of his good will, because He always has special regard for a good will. And when a man is lawfully hindered, he ought to have a good will and a humble intention to receive Holy Communion, and so he will not lack the fruit of the Sacrament.

Truly, every devout man can, every day and every hour, retire savingly and without prohibition into a spiritual communion with Christ, that is to say, into a remembrance of His Passion. A man communicates mystically and invisibly as often as he remembers devoutly the mystery of the Incarnation of Christ and His sufferings, and by them is enkindled into His love. Nevertheless, on certain days and times, a man is bound to receive sacramentally the Body of his Redeemer with great reverence, and to seek in the reception the praise and honor of God more than his own consolation. But he who prepares himself for no other reason than that a feast is coming, or that custom compels him to it, will commonly be unready for it. He therefore is blessed who, as often as he says Mass or communicates, offers himself truly to our Lord in holy sacrifice.

In saying Mass, do not be overlong or overbrief, but keep the good middle way, as they do with whom you live, for you ought not do what would burden others or make them weary, but to keep the ordinary way, after the ordinance of the holy Fathers, and to conform yourself to all that will be profitable to others rather than to follow your own devotion or private pleasure.

11. *That the Body of Christ and Holy Scripture Are Most Necessary for the Health of Man's Soul*

O Lord Jesus, how great sweetness it is to a devout soul when he is fed by You at your heavenly feast where no other food is served except Yourself, his only Beloved, who are most excellent to him above all the desires of his heart. Truly, it should be sweet and pleasant to me to weep before You with an interior and humble affection, and with the blessed woman Mary Magdalene to wash Your feet with the tears of my eyes. But where is that devotion? Where is that copious shedding of holy tears?

Certainly, all my heart ought to burn and weep for joy at the sight of You and Your holy angels, for I truly have You present with me, though You are hid under another appearance. My eyes could not bear to behold You in Your own divine brightness, nor could all the world bear to see You in the light and glory of Your majesty. Therefore You greatly help my weakness by hiding Yourself under this Holy Sacrament. I truly have Him and worship Him whom the angels worship in heaven, but I only by faith and they in open sight and in His own unhidden likeness. It behooves me to be content with the light of true faith and to walk in it until the day of everlasting light will appear and the shadow of images will pass away. When what is perfect shall come, all use of the sacraments will cease, for they who are blessed in the heavenly glory have no need of this sacramental medicine. They joy without end in the presence of God, beholding His glory face to face, and, transformed from brightness to brightness by the Godhead, they taste the glory of the Son of God made man as He was from the beginning, and will be forever.

When I remember all these marvelous comforts, whatever solace I have in this world, even though it be spiritual, becomes grievous and tedious to me. As long as I do not see my Lord clearly in His glory, I count as nothing all that I see and hear in this world. Lord, You are my witness that nothing can comfort me, nor any creature give me rest, save You, my Lord God, whom I desire to see and behold eternally. But that is not possible for me as long as I am in this mortal life. Wherefore, it behooves me to keep myself in great patience and to submit myself to You in everything I desire. Your holy saints who now rejoice with You awaited the coming of Your glory in good faith and patience all the time they lived here. What they believed I believe; what they hoped to have I hope to have; where by Your grace they arrived I trust to come. Until then I walk in faith and take comfort from the examples of the saints. I have holy books, also, for my solace, to look upon as a mirror of life, and above all these I have for a singular remedy Your Holy Sacrament.

I perceive well that there are two things most necessary for me in this world, without which this miserable life would be insupportable. As long as I am in this body, I confess myself to have need of two things, that is to say, food and light, and these two you have given me. You have given the Blessed Sacrament for the refreshment of my soul and body, and You have set Your word as a lantern before my feet to show me the way I shall go. Without these two I cannot live well, for the Word of God is the light of my soul, and this Sacrament is the bread of my life.

These two can be called the two tables, set here and there in the spiritual treasure of holy Church. The one is the table of the holy altar, having the living Bread that is the precious Body of Christ; the other is the table of the laws of God, containing the holy doctrine which instructs man in the right faith and in the true belief and leads him into the *sancta sanctorum*, where the inward secrets of Scripture are hidden and contained. I give You thanks, my Lord Jesus, the Brightness of eternal light, for this table of holy doctrine You have ministered to us by Your servants, the doctors, prophets, and Apostles. And thanks also to You, Creator and Redeemer of mankind, that, to show all the world the greatness of Your charity, You have prepared a great supper in which You do not set forth the lamb that was the type in the Old Law, but Your holy Body and Blood to be taken, thereby making all faithful people glad in that sacred feast, and giving them to drink of Your chalice of salvation, in which is contained with abundant sweetness all the delights of paradise, where angels eat with us.

Oh, how great and how honorable is the office of priests, to whom is given the power to consecrate, with the holy words of consecration, the Lord of all majesty, to bless Him with their lips, to hold Him in their hands, to receive Him into their mouths, and to administer Him to others. Oh, how clean should be the hands, how pure the mouth, how holy the body, and how undefiled the heart of a priest, into whom so often the Author of all purity enters. Truly, there should proceed from the mouth of a priest, who so often receives the Sacrament of Christ, no word but what is holy, honest, and profitable. His eyes, accustomed to behold the Body of Christ, should be holy, simple, and chaste. His hands, accustomed to touch the Creator of heaven and earth, should be holy, pure, and lifted up to heaven. Therefore, it is especially said to priests in the Old Law: Be you holy, for I, your Lord God, am holy.

O Almighty God, may Your grace be with us and help us, who have received the office of priesthood, so that we may serve You worthily and devoutly in all purity, and though we may not live in as great innocence as we ought, yet give us at least the grace to weep in sorrow for the evils we have done, so that in spiritual humility and a full purpose of good will we may serve You hereafter.

12. *That He Who Would Receive Communion Ought to Prepare Himself for It with Great Diligence*

I am the Lover of all purity, and the generous Giver of all holiness. I seek a pure heart, and there is My resting place. Make ready for Me a great chamber, strewn with rushes—that is, your heart, and with My disciples I shall keep My Easter with you. If you desire that I should come to you and dwell with you, free yourself of the old filth of sin and cleanse also the habitation of your heart. Exclude the world and all the clamorous noise of sin, and sit solitary as a sparrow on the eaves of a house, and think upon your own offenses with great bitterness of heart, for a true lover will prepare for his beloved the best and the fairest place he can, for that is a sign of the love and affection of him who receives his friends. Nevertheless, I know that you cannot, by yourself, make this preparation fully as it ought to be in every point, though you were to go about it for a whole year together and had nothing else in your mind to think about. By My mercy and grace alone you are allowed to go to My table, as if a poor man were called to the dinner of a rich man and had nothing to give him in return, save only to humble himself and thank him. Do this as far as you can with your best diligence and do not do it out of custom only, or out of necessity only, because you are bound to it, but out of awe and reverence and great affection. Receive the Body of your beloved Lord God who so lovingly deigns to come to you. I am He who has called you; I have commanded this thing to be done;

I will supply whatever is wanting in you. Come, therefore, and receive Me.

When I give you the grace of devotion, give thanks to Me for it—not because you are worthy to have it, but because I have shown My mercy lovingly toward you. And if you do not have the grace of devotion through the reception of this Sacrament, but feel yourself even dryer and less devout than before, continue on in your prayer. Bewail, weep, and call for mercy, and do not cease until you have received some little drop of this healthful grace of devotion. You have need of Me; I do not have need of you. You do not come to sanctify Me, but I come to sanctify you and to make you better than you were before. You come to be sanctified and united to Me and to receive new grace and to be kindled anew to amendment. Do not forget this grace, but always, with all your diligence, prepare your heart, and bring your Beloved unto you.

It behooves you not only to prepare yourself for devotion before you have received Communion, but also to keep yourself diligently in it after receiving. And it is no less requisite to keep devotion afterwards than to prepare devoutly before, for a good keeping of devotion afterwards is the best preparation to receive new grace. And a man will be the more indisposed to new grace if, after he has received the Sacrament, he gives himself straightway to outward consolation. Beware of much speaking, abide in some secret place, and keep yourself with your Lord God, for you have Him whom all the world cannot take from you. I am He to whom you must give all, so that from henceforth you live, not for yourself, but only for Me.

13. *That a Devout Soul Should Greatly Desire with All His Heart to be Made One with Christ in the Blessed Sacrament*

Who will grant me, Lord, to find You only, and open all my heart to You, and have You as my heart's desire, so that no man may deceive me, nor any creature move me or draw me back, but that You alone speak to me, and I to you, as a lover is wont to speak to his beloved, and a friend to his beloved friend. This is what I pray for, this is what I desire, that I may be joined wholly to You and that I may withdraw my heart from all created things, and that through Holy Communion and the frequent saying of Mass I may savor and taste eternal things. O Lord God, when shall I be made one with You and wholly melted into Your love, so that I may wholly forget myself? Be in me, and may I be in You, and grant that we may always so abide, always together in one.

Truly, You are my Beloved, elected and chosen before all others, in whom my soul desires to abide all the days of my life. You are the Lord of peace, in whom is sovereign peace and true rest, and without whom is labor and sorrow and infinite misery. Truly, you are the hidden God, and your counsel is not with wicked people, but with humble men and the simple at heart.

Oh, how sweet and kind is Your Holy Spirit, who, to the end that You might show Your chosen people Your sweetness, vouchsafes to refresh them with the most sweet Bread that comes down from heaven. Truly, there is no other nation so great that has its God so nigh to it as you, Lord God, are close to all Your faithful people, to whom You give Yourself as meat and drink as their daily solace, and to raise their hearts to the love of heavenly things. Oh, what people is there so noble as the Christian people, or what creature under heaven is so much beloved as the devout Christian soul whom God feeds with His own glorious Flesh and Blood? O inestimable grace, O marvelous worthiness, O love without measure, singularly shown to man. But what return shall I make to God for this grace and for all this high charity? Truly, there is nothing more acceptable to Him than to give Him my heart wholly and inwardly join myself to Him. Then will all my heart rejoice, when my soul is made perfectly one with Him. Then will He say to me: If you will be with Me, I will be with you. And I will respond and say: Vouchsafe, Lord, to abide with me, and I will gladly abide with You, for all my desire is that my heart may be close knit to You without separation.

14. Of the Burning Desire That Some Devout Persons Had for the Body of Christ

Oh, how multitudinous is the sweetness, Lord, that you have hid for those who fear You! But what is it for those who love You? Truly, when I recall many devout persons who have come to the Holy Sacrament with great fervor of devotion, I am many times astonished and confounded within myself that I go to Your altar and to the table of Your Holy Communion so coldly and with so little fervor; that I remain so dry and without any affection of heart; and that I am not so completely kindled before You, my Lord God, nor so strongly drawn to You in affection as many devout persons have been who, because of the great desire they have had for Holy Communion and because of the manifest love of heart they have had toward it, could not refrain themselves from weeping, but earnestly, with heart and soul together, received You, Lord, because they could not otherwise satisfy or temper their hunger, unless they took Your Holy Sacrament as they did, with great joy and spiritual gladness. Truly, their great burning faith is a sign and a token of Your holy presence, and they truly knew their Lord in the breaking of bread, whose heart so strongly burned in them at the presence of their Lord Jesus, who was then walking with them. But truly, such affection and devotion and such strong fervor and love are oftentimes far from me. Be, therefore, most sweet and kind Lord Jesus, be merciful and mild unto me, and grant me, Your poorest servant, sometimes to feel some little spark of the great affection of Your love in this Holy Communion, so that my faith may the more recover and amend, and my hope, through Your goodness, be more perfect, and my charity, being once perfectly kindled and having experience of the heavenly manna, never fail.

Your mercy, Lord, is strong enough to grant me this grace I so much desire, and, when the time of Your pleasure shall come, to visit me kindly with the spirit of a burning fervor to You. And though I do not burn with such fervor as such especially devout persons have done, I nevertheless desire by Your grace to be inflamed by that burning desire, praying and hoping that I may be made a companion of all such fervent lovers and be numbered in their holy company.

15. *That the Grace of Devotion Is Gained through Humility and Forsaking Ourselves*

It behooves you constantly to seek the grace of devotion, without ceasing to ask for it, patiently and faithfully to await it, thankfully to receive it, humbly to keep it, zealously to work with it, and wholly to commit to God the time and manner of His heavenly visitation until it be His pleasure to come to you. Above all, you ought to humble yourself when you feel but little inward devotion, but you should not be too much cast down or too desolate, for our Lord often gives in a short moment what He has denied for a long time before. Moreover, sometimes at the end of prayer He gives what at its beginning He delayed granting.

If grace should always immediately be granted and should straightway be present according to the will of him who asks for it, it could not be borne by a weak and feeble person. Therefore, the grace of devotion is to be awaited and expected in good hope and in humble patience, and you ought to impute it to yourself and to your own sins when grace is not given or is suddenly taken away from you. Sometimes, it is but a little thing that prevents or conceals grace, if, indeed, that can be called a little thing and not a great thing that hinders and forestalls so good a thing. But whether it is little or great, if you remove it and perfectly overcome it, then what you desire will be granted you. And as soon as you betake yourself with all your heart to God, and desire neither this thing nor that thing for your own pleasure, but wholly submit your will to His will, you will find yourself united to Him and put in great inward peace, for nothing will taste so good to you or please you more than that the will of God be fully done in you.

Whoever, therefore, with a pure, simple heart lifts his intention up to God and empties out of himself all inordinate love or displeasure over any worldly thing will be the more ready to receive grace and will be the best worthy to have the gift of devotion. Where our Lord finds the vessel empty and void, there He gives His blessing, and the more perfectly a man can renounce himself and all the worldly things, and by despising himself can the more die to himself, so much the sooner will grace come and enter more plenteously into him and lift his heart higher unto God. Then his heart will see and be rich, and will marvel and be dilated within him, for the grace of our Lord is with him and he has completely put himself into His hand forever. Lo, in such a manner will a man be blessed who seeks God with all his heart and does not set his mind on vanities. Such a man in receiving the Holy Sacrament deserves great grace of union in God, for he looks not to his own devotion and consolation, but to the glory and honor of God.

16. *That We Should Reveal All Our Necessities to Christ and Ask His Grace*

O most sweet Lord whom I desire devoutly to receive, You know the infirmity and the need in which I am. You know in how many sins and vices I lie, how often I am grieved, tempted, troubled, and defiled. I come to You for remedy and make my prayer to You for comfort. I speak to Him who knows all things, to whom all my secret and inward thoughts are manifest and open, and who alone can perfectly counsel and help me. You know what I need and how poor I am in virtue.

Lo, I stand before You poor and naked, desiring and asking Your grace. Refresh me, therefore, Your poorest servant who begs for spiritual food, kindle my heart with the fire of Your love, and illumine my blindness by the light of Your presence. Turn all worldly things into bitterness to me, all grievous and irritating things into patience, and all created things into a despising and a forgetfulness of them. Lift up my heart to You in heaven, and do not permit me to live vainly or to err in this world. You, O Lord, will from henceforth be sweet to me forever, for You alone are my meat and drink, my love, my joy, my sweetness and all my goodness.

Would God that You would enkindle me, enflame me, and turn me wholly to Yourself, so that I may be made one spirit with You by the grace of inward union and by a melting into You of burning love. Permit me not to depart from You fasting and thirsty, but work with me mercifully, as you have often marvelously worked with your beloved servants in times past. What marvel would it be if I were all enflamed in You, yet failed within myself, since You are the fire always burning and never failing, the love purifying the heart and enlightening the understanding of all Your creatures.

17. *Of the Burning Love and Great Affection We Should Have in Receiving Christ*

With high devotion and with burning love and with all due affection of the heart, I desire to receive You, Lord, as many saints and devout persons who most pleased You by the holiness of their life and were in most burning devotion to You have desired You in their Communions. O my Lord God, my love eternal, all my goodness and felicity without ending, I desire to receive You with as great desire and as due reverence as any holy man ever did or might do.

And though I am unworthy to have such feelings of devotion as they had, I offer You the whole affection of my heart as truly as if I alone had all the burning and flaming desires they ever had. And above all, I give and offer You with high reverence and worship and inward fervor all that a humble mind can imagine and desire. I desire to reserve nothing for myself, but I offer You in sacrifice, freely and most liberally, myself and all that is mine, and also, my Lord God, my Creator and Redeemer, I desire to receive You this day with such affection, reverence, praise, and honor, and with such thanks, dignity, and love, and with such faith, hope, and purity as Your most holy and glorious Mother, the Virgin Mary, desired and received You when she meekly and devoutly answered the angel who showed her the mystery of her Incarnation and said: *Ecce ancilla Domini, fiat mihi secundum verbum tuum*, which is to say: Lo, I am the handmaid of God, be it done to me according to your word.

As Your blessed precursor, St. John the Baptist, most excellent of all saints, was glad and rejoiced with great joy in the Holy Spirit through Your presence when he was yet in his mother's womb, and afterwards when he saw You walking among the people, meekly and with devout affection, said: The friend of the spouse, who stands and hears, rejoices with great joy to hear the voice of the spouse. So do I desire to be inflamed with a great and holy desire and to present myself to You with all my heart.

Wherefore, I offer and yield to You also all the praise of devout hearts, the burning affections, the enraptured thoughts, the spiritual illuminations, the heavenly visions, with all virtues and praising done or to be done by any creature in heaven or on earth, for me and for all them who are committed to my prayers, that You may be worthily praised and glorified forever. Accept, Lord God, the manifold praises and blessings which are rightfully due to You from me, according to the multitude of Your greatness, more than can be spoken. All these I yield to You and desire to yield to You every day and every moment, and with all my desire and affection I humbly exhort and pray all the heavenly spirits and all faithful people to yield to You with me due thanks and praise.

I beseech You that all people, tribes, and tongues may magnify Your holy and most sweet Name with great joy and burning devotion, and that all who devoutly and reverently administer this most high Sacrament, or with full faith receive it, may by it deserve to find before You grace and mercy, and that, when they have obtained the devotion they desire and are spiritually made one with You and thereby well comforted and marvelously refreshed, they will have me, poor sinner, in their remembrance.

18. *That a Man Should Not Be a Curious Searcher into the Holy Sacrament, but a Humble Follower of Christ, Always Subduing His Reason to the Faith*

You must beware of curious and unprofitable searching into this most profound Sacrament, if you would not be drowned in the great depths of doubt. He who inquires too much about God's majesty will soon thrust out glory. God has power to work much more than man can understand. However, a meek and humble inquiry after the truth, ready always to be taught and to walk after the teachings of the holy Fathers, is permissible. Blessed is that simplicity that leaves the way of hard questions and goes in the plain and certain way of the commandments of God.

Many have lost their devotion because they would search higher things than pertained to them. Faith and a good life are asked of you, not height of understanding or the depths of the mysteries of God. If you cannot understand or grasp such things as are within you, how can you then comprehend those things that are above you? Submit yourself, therefore, humbly to God and submit your reason also to faith, and the light of knowledge and of true understanding will be given to you as shall be most profitable and necessary. Some are grievously tempted in faith in the Blessed Sacrament, but that is not to be imputed to them, but, rather, to the enemy. Therefore, give him no heed. Do not dispute with your thoughts and do not answer to the doubts your enemy will lay before you. But believe the words of God, and believe His saints and prophets, and the wicked enemy will soon flee from you. It is often very profitable that the servants of God should feel and bear such doubts for their more certain testing. The enemy commonly does not tempt unfaithful people and sinners of whom he has sure possession; rather, he tempts and vexes the faithful and the devout in different manners.

Go, therefore, with a pure and undoubting faith and proceed to this Sacrament with humble reverence. Commit faithfully to God whatever you cannot understand, for God will not deceive you; but he who trusts overmuch to himself will be deceived. God walks with simple people, He shows himself to humble persons, He gives understanding to those who are poor in spirit, He opens wisdom to pure, clean minds, but He hides His grace from inquisitive and proud men. Man's reason is humble and weak and soon deceived, but faith is firm and true and cannot be deceived.

If the words of God were such that they might be easily understood by man's reason, they would not be so marvelous and so inestimable as they are. Oh, the eternal God and the Lord of infinite power does great things in heaven and on earth that cannot be investigated. Therefore, all reason and all natural effort must follow faith without further questioning, for faith and love in this most Holy and most excellent Sacrament excel and work, high above all reason, in ways unsearchable.